THE ALL-SUMMER COOKBOOK

THE All-Summer COOKBOOK

SMITHMARK

This edition published in 1996
by Smithmark Publishers,
a division of U.S. Media Holdings, Inc.,
16 East 32nd Street
New York
NY 10016

SMITHMARK books are available for bulk purchase for sales promotion
and premium use. For details write or call the Manager of Special Sales,
SMITHMARK Publishers
16 East 32nd Street
New York
NY 10016
(212) 532-6600

ISBN 0 8317 5945 3

Contributing authors: Catherine Atkinson, Maxine Clarke, Christine France,
Shirley Gill, Carole Handslip, Sue Maggs, Annie Nichols,
Jenny Stacey, Liz Trigg and Steven Wheeler

Publisher: Joanna Lorenz
Senior Cookery Editor: Linda Fraser
Assistant Editor: Emma Brown
Designer: Siân Keogh
Photographers: Karl Adamson, Edward Allright, James Duncan,
Michelle Garrett and Don Last
Stylists: Madeleine Brehaut, Hilary Guy and Fiona Tillett

Printed and bound in Hong Kong

The material in this book previously appeared as individual
titles in the *Step-by-Step* series.

10 9 8 7 6 5 4 3 2 1

CONTENTS

INTRODUCTION

Summer is a wonderful season for the cook. At no other time of year is a more diverse and appealing assortment of fresh natural produce available. From the freshest hand-picked berries and seasonal fruits to delicious sun-ripened vegetables and pungent garden herbs, all can be used to create a wonderful variety of sumptous summer fare.

Whatever the occasion, from picnics to summer lunches, barbecues to garden parties, this inspiring collection is sure to provide the perfect dish. The chapters include delicious soups and light meals, spectacular salads, barbecue and picnic recipes, all sorts of pasta dishes, breads and pizzas, and, of course, summer desserts. In addition to classics such as Salade Niçoise, Tandoori Chicken, and Margherita Pizza, there are also exciting innovative recipes featuring some favorite ingredients: try Red Pepper and Watercress Filo Parcels, Warm Duck Salad with Orange and Cilantro, and Salmon with Spicy Pesto. If you enjoy looking far afield for inspiration, you will find plenty here to please. There are lots of recipes from around the world, for example, Broiled Chicken with Pica De Gallo Salsa, Vietnamese Stuffed Squid, and Russian Salad.

All the recipes use high-quality, fresh produce and, from the simplest soup to the most contemporary salad, reflect and encapsulate the essence of summer. With so many wonderful ingredients to choose from, this tempting collection of recipes is sure to inspire, and the simple-to-follow, step-by-step format means that creating enticing summer meals becomes easy and enjoyable.

Pasta Shells with Tomatoes and Arugula

This pretty-colored pasta dish relies for its success on a salad green called arugula. Available in large supermarkets, it is a leaf easily grown in the garden or a window box and tastes slightly peppery.

Serves 4

INGREDIENTS
1 lb shell pasta
salt and pepper
1 lb very ripe cherry tomatoes
3 tbsp olive oil
3 oz fresh arugula
Parmesan cheese

olive oil

pasta shells

cherry tomatoes

arugula

Parmesan cheese

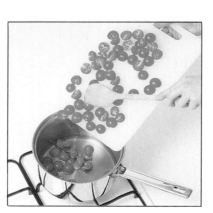

1 Cook the pasta in plenty of boiling salted water according to the manufacturer's instructions. Drain well.

2 Halve the tomatoes. Trim, wash, and dry the arugula.

3 Heat the oil in a large saucepan, add the tomatoes, and cook for barely 1 minute. The tomatoes should only just heat through and not disintegrate.

4 Shave the Parmesan cheese using a rotary vegetable peeler.

5 Add the pasta, then the arugula. Carefully stir to mix and heat through. Season well with salt and freshly ground black pepper. Serve immediately with plenty of shaved Parmesan cheese.

Red Pepper and Watercress Filo Parcels

Peppery watercress combines well with sweet red pepper in these crisp little parcels.

Makes 8

INGREDIENTS
3 red peppers
6 oz watercress
1 cup ricotta cheese
¼ cup blanched almonds, toasted and chopped
salt and freshly ground black pepper
8 sheets of filo pastry
2 tbsp olive oil

ricotta

red pepper

watercress

almonds

filo pastry

1 Preheat the oven to 375°F. Place the peppers under a hot broiler until blistered and charred. Place in a paper bag. When cool enough to handle peel, seed and pat dry on kitchen paper.

2 Place the peppers and watercress in a food processor and pulse until coarsely chopped. Spoon into a bowl.

3 Mix in the ricotta and almonds, and season to taste.

4 Working with 1 sheet of filo pastry at a time, cut out 2 × 7 in and 2 × 2 in squares from each sheet. Brush 1 large square with a little olive oil and place a second large square at an angle of 90 degrees to form a star shape.

5 Place 1 of the small squares in the center of the star shape, brush lightly with oil and top with a second small square.

6 Top with ⅛ of the red pepper mixture. Bring the edges together to form a purse shape and twist to seal. Place on a lightly greased cookie sheet and cook for 25–30 minutes until golden.

Tagliatelle with Pea Sauce, Asparagus and Broad Beans

A creamy pea sauce makes a wonderful combination with the crunchy young vegetables.

Serves 4

INGREDIENTS
1 tbsp olive oil
1 garlic clove, crushed
6 scallions, sliced
1 cup fresh or frozen baby peas, defrosted
12 oz fresh young asparagus
2 tbsp chopped fresh sage, plus extra leaves, to garnish
finely grated rind of 2 lemons
1¾ cups fresh vegetable stock or water
8 oz fresh or frozen broad beans, defrosted
1 lb tagliatelle
4 tbsp low-fat yogurt

lemon

garlic

asparagus

broad beans

peas

yogurt

tagliatelle

sage

scallions

1 Heat the oil in a pan. Add the garlic and scallions and cook gently for 2–3 minutes until softened.

2 Add the peas and ⅓ of the asparagus, together with the sage, lemon rind and stock or water. Bring to a boil, reduce the heat and simmer for 10 minutes until tender. Purée in a blender until smooth.

3 Meanwhile remove the outer skins from the broad beans and discard.

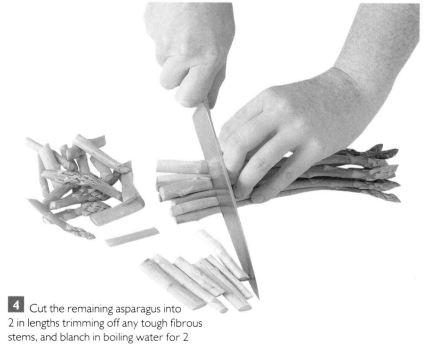

4 Cut the remaining asparagus into 2 in lengths trimming off any tough fibrous stems, and blanch in boiling water for 2 minutes.

5 Cook the tagliatelle following the instructions on the side of the package until *al dente*. Drain well.

COOK'S TIP

Frozen peas and beans have been suggested here to cut down the preparation time, but the dish tastes even better if you use fresh young vegetables when in season.

6 Add the cooked asparagus and shelled beans to the sauce and reheat. Stir in the yogurt and toss into the tagliatelle. Garnish with a few extra sage leaves and serve.

Polenta and Baked Tomatoes

A staple of northern Italy, polenta is a nourishing, filling food, served here with a delicious fresh tomato and olive topping.

Serves 4–6

INGREDIENTS
9 cups water
1 ¼ lb quick-cooking polenta
12 large ripe plum tomatoes, sliced
4 garlic cloves, thinly sliced
2 tbsp chopped fresh oregano or
  marjoram
½ cup black olives, pitted
salt and freshly ground black pepper
2 tbsp olive oil

black olives

marjoram

plum tomatoes

garlic

oregano

polenta

1 Place the water in a large saucepan and bring to a boil. Whisk in the polenta and simmer for 5 minutes.

2 Remove the pan from the heat and pour the thickened polenta into a 9 in × 13 in jelly roll pan. Smooth out the surface with a spatula until level, and leave to cool.

3 Preheat the oven to 350°F. With a 3 in round pastry cutter, stamp out 12 rounds of polenta. Lay them so that they slightly overlap in a lightly oiled ovenproof dish.

4 Layer the tomatoes, garlic, oregano or marjoram and olives on top of the polenta, seasoning the layers as you go. Sprinkle with the olive oil, and bake uncovered for 30–35 minutes. Serve immediately.

Smoked Salmon Pâté

Making this pâté in individual ramekins wrapped in extra smoked salmon gives an extra special presentation. Taste the mousse as you are making it as some people prefer more lemon juice and seasoning.

Serves 4

INGREDIENTS
¾lb thinly sliced smoked
   salmon
⅔ cup heavy cream
finely grated rind and juice of 1 lemon
salt and freshly ground black pepper
melba toast, to serve

smoked salmon

lemon

black pepper

salt

1 Line four small ramekin dishes with plastic wrap. Line the dishes with 4 oz of the smoked salmon cut into strips long enough to flop over the edges.

2 In a food processor fitted with a metal blade, process the rest of the salmon with the seasoning, heavy cream and lemon rind and juice.

3 Pack the lined ramekins with the smoked salmon pâté and wrap over the loose strips of salmon. Cover and chill for 30 minutes, then turn out of the molds and serve with melba toast.

COOK'S TIP

Process the salmon in short bursts until it is just smooth. Don't over-process the pâté or it will thicken too much.

Baked Herb Crêpes

These mouth-watering, light herb crêpes make a striking starter at a dinner party, but are equally splendid served with a crisp salad for lunch.

Serves 4

INGREDIENTS
2 tbsp chopped fresh herbs
  (e.g. parsley, thyme, and chervil)
1 tbsp sunflower oil, plus extra for
  frying
½ cup skim milk
3 eggs
¼ cup flour
pinch of salt
1 tbsp olive oil

FOR THE SAUCE
2 tbsp olive oil
1 small onion, chopped
2 garlic cloves, crushed
1 tbsp grated fresh ginger root
1 × 14 oz can chopped tomatoes

FOR THE FILLING
1 lb fresh spinach
¾ cup ricotta cheese
2 tbsp pine nuts, toasted
5 halves sun-dried tomatoes in olive
  oil, drained and chopped
2 tbsp shredded fresh basil
salt, nutmeg and freshly ground black
  pepper
4 egg whites

1 To make the crêpes, place the herbs and oil in a blender and blend until smooth, pushing down any whole pieces with a spatula. Add the milk, eggs, flour and salt and process again until smooth and pale green. Leave to rest for 30 minutes.

onion

parsley

ginger root

chopped tomatoes

spinach

sun-dried tomatoes

garlic

nutmeg

thyme

flour

egg

skim milk

2 Heat a small non-stick crêpe or frying pan and add a very small amount of oil. Pour out any excess oil and pour in a ladleful of the batter. Swirl around to cover the base. Cook for 1–2 minutes, turn over and cook the other side. Repeat with the remaining batter to make 8 crêpes.

3 To make the sauce, heat the oil in a small pan. Add the onion, garlic and ginger and cook gently for 5 minutes until softened. Add the tomatoes and cook for a further 10–15 minutes until the mixture thickens. Purée in a blender, sieve and set aside.

4 To make the filling, wash the spinach, removing any large stalks, and place in a large pan with only the water that clings to the leaves. Cover and cook, stirring once, until the spinach has just wilted. Remove from the heat and refresh in cold water. Place in a sieve or colander, squeeze out the excess water and chop finely. Mix the spinach with the ricotta, pine nuts, sun-dried tomatoes and basil. Season with salt, nutmeg and freshly ground black pepper.

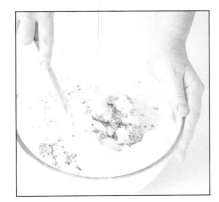

5 Preheat the oven to 375°F. Whisk the 4 egg whites until they form stiff peaks but are not dry. Fold ⅓ into the spinach and ricotta to lighten the mixture, then gently fold in the rest.

6 Taking one crêpe at a time, place on a lightly oiled cookie sheet. Place a large spoonful of filling on each one and fold into quarters. Repeat until all the filling and crêpes are used up. Bake in the oven for 10–15 minutes or until set. Reheat the tomato sauce to serve with the crêpes.

COOK'S TIP

If preferred, use plain sun-dried tomatoes without any oil, and soak them in warm water for 20 minutes before using.

Ceviche

This is a hot and sweet starter of marinated fresh fish. Take very special care in choosing the fish for this dish; it must be as fresh as possible and served on the same day it is made.

Serves 6

INGREDIENTS

12 oz medium cooked shrimp
12 oz scallops, removed from their
   shells, with corals intact if possible
12 oz salmon fillet
6 oz tomatoes
1 × 6 oz mango
1 red onion, finely chopped
1 fresh red chili
juice of 8 limes
2 tbsp sugar
2 pink grapefruits
3 oranges
4 limes
salt and freshly ground black pepper

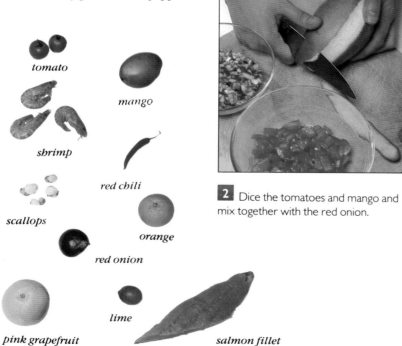

tomato

mango

shrimp

red chili

scallops

orange

red onion

pink grapefruit

lime

salmon fillet

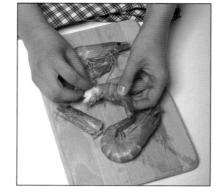

1 Peel the shrimp and cut the scallops into ½ in dice.

2 Dice the tomatoes and mango and mix together with the red onion.

3 Cut the fish into small pieces, dice the chili and mix with the fish, tomato and mango. Add the lime juice, sugar and seasoning. Stir and leave to marinate for 3 hours.

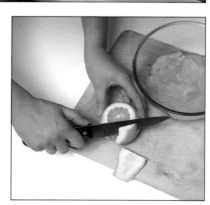

4 Segment the grapefruit, oranges and limes. Drain off as much excess lime juice as possible and mix the fruit segments into the marinated ingredients. Season to taste and serve.

Clam Chowder

Canned clams if necessary, once drained, can be used as an alternative to fresh ones in their shells. During cooking, if any of the clam shells remain closed, discard them as they would have been dead before cooking.

Serves 4

INGREDIENTS

1¼ cups heavy cream
6 tbsp unsalted butter
1 small onion, finely chopped
  (optional)
1 apple, sliced
1 garlic clove, crushed
3 tbsp mild curry powder
12 oz baby corn
2½ cups fish stock
8 oz new potatoes, peeled and
  cooked
24 pearl onions, peeled and boiled
40 small clams
salt and freshly ground black pepper
8 lime wedges, to garnish

baby onions

potato

lime

curry powder

clams

apple

baby corn

1 Pour the cream into a small saucepan and cook over a high heat until it is reduced by half.

2 In a larger pan, melt half the butter. Add the onion, apple, garlic clove and curry powder. Sauté until the onion is translucent. Add the reduced cream and stir well.

3 In another saucepan, melt the remaining butter and add the baby corn. Cook for 5 minutes. Increase the heat and add the cream mixture and stock. Bring to a boil.

4 Add the potatoes, pearl onions and clams. Cover and cook until the clams have opened. Discard any that do not open. Season well to taste, and serve garnished with lime wedges.

Salade Niçoise

Salade Niçoise is the happy marriage of tuna fish, hard-cooked eggs, green beans, and potatoes. Anchovies, olives, and capers are often also included, but it is the first four ingredients that combine to make this a classic salad.

Serves 4

INGREDIENTS
1½ lb potatoes, peeled
salt and pepper
½ lb green beans, trimmed and
    stringed
3 eggs, hard-cooked
1 romaine lettuce
½ cup French Dressing
½ lb small plum tomatoes, quartered
14 oz canned albacore tuna in oil,
    drained
1 oz canned anchovies
2 tbsp capers
12 black olives

2 Slice the potatoes thickly. Shell and quarter the eggs.

3 Wash the lettuce and spin dry, then chop the leaves roughly. Toss with half of the dressing in a large salad bowl.

1 Bring the potatoes to a boil in salted water and cook for 20 minutes. Boil the green beans for 6 minutes. Drain and cool the potatoes and beans under running water.

romaine lettuce

green beans

olives

anchovies

potatoes

plum tomatoes

capers

4 Toss the potatoes, green beans, and tomatoes with dressing, then scatter over the salad leaves.

COOK'S TIP
The ingredients for Salade Niçoise can be prepared well in advance and should be assembled just before serving to retain flavor and freshness.

5 Break the tuna fish up with a fork and distribute over the salad with the anchovies, capers, and olives. Season to taste and serve.

Melon and Basil Soup

A deliciously refreshing, chilled fruit soup, just right for a hot summer's day.

Serves 4–6

INGREDIENTS
2 canteloupe or honeydew melons
⅓ cup superfine sugar
¾ cup water
finely grated zest and juice of 1 lime
3 tbsp shredded fresh basil
fresh basil leaves, to garnish

basil

sugar

lime

melon

1 Cut the melons in half across the middle. Scrape out the seeds and discard. Using a melon baller, scoop out 20–24 balls and set aside for the garnish. Scoop out the remaining flesh and place in a blender or food processor.

2 Place the sugar, water and lime zest in a small pan over a low heat. Stir until dissolved, bring to the boil and simmer for 2–3 minutes. Remove from the heat and leave to cool slightly. Pour half the mixture into the blender or food processor with the melon flesh. Blend until smooth, adding the remaining syrup and lime juice to taste.

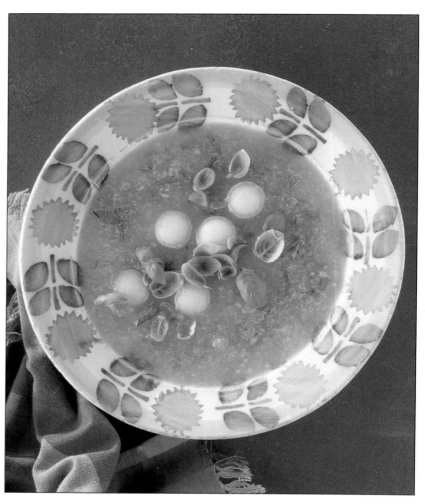

3 Pour the mixture into a bowl, stir in the basil and chill. Serve garnished with basil leaves and melon balls.

COOK'S TIP

Add the syrup in two stages, as the amount of sugar needed will depend on the sweetness of the melon.

Chilled Fresh Tomato Soup

This effortless uncooked soup can be made in minutes.

Serves 4–6

INGREDIENTS

3–3½ lb ripe tomatoes, peeled and
 roughly chopped
4 garlic cloves, crushed
2 tbsp extra-virgin olive oil (optional)
2 tbsp balsamic vinegar
freshly ground black pepper
4 slices wholewheat bread
low-fat ricotta cheese, to garnish

wholewheat bread

garlic

ricotta cheese

peppercorns

tomato

COOK'S TIP

For the best flavor, it is important to
use only fully ripened, succulent
tomatoes in this soup.

1 Place the tomatoes in a blender with the garlic and olive oil if using. Blend until smooth.

2 Pass the mixture through a sieve to remove the seeds. Stir in the balsamic vinegar and season to taste with pepper. Leave in the fridge to chill.

3 Toast the bread lightly on both sides. While still hot, cut off the crusts and slice in half horizontally. Place the toast on a board with the uncooked sides facing down and, using a circular motion, rub to remove any doughy pieces of bread.

4 Cut each slice into 4 triangles. Place on a griddle and toast the uncooked sides until lightly golden. Garnish each bowl of soup with a spoonful of ricotta cheese and serve with the melba toast.

Avocado, Tomato, and Mozzarella Pasta Salad with Pine Nuts

A salad made from ingredients representing the colors of the Italian flag – a sunny cheerful dish!

Serves 4

INGREDIENTS
1 ½ cups pasta bows (farfalle)
6 ripe red tomatoes
½ lb mozzarella cheese
1 large ripe avocado
2 tbsp pine nuts, toasted
1 sprig fresh basil, to garnish

DRESSING
6 tbsp olive oil
2 tbsp wine vinegar
1 tsp balsamic vinegar (optional)
1 tsp whole-grain mustard
pinch of sugar
salt and pepper
2 tbsp chopped fresh basil

olive oil

avocado

tomatoes

basil

mozzarella cheese

pine nuts   *pasta bows*

1 Cook the pasta in plenty of boiling salted water according to the manufacturer's instructions. Drain well and cool.

2 Slice the tomatoes and mozzarella cheese into thin rounds.

3 Halve the avocado, remove the pit, and peel off the skin. Slice the flesh lengthwise.

4 Whisk all the dressing ingredients together in a small bowl.

5 Arrange the tomato, mozzarella, and avocado in overlapping slices around the edge of a flat plate.

6 Toss the pasta with half the dressing and the chopped basil. Pile into the center of the plate. Pour over the remaining dressing, scatter over the pine nuts, and garnish with a sprig of fresh basil. Serve immediately.

Cucumber and Alfalfa Tortillas

Wheat tortillas are extremely simple to prepare at home. Served with a crisp, fresh salsa, they make a marvelous light lunch or supper dish.

Serves 4

INGREDIENTS
2 cups flour, sifted
pinch of salt
3 tbsp olive oil
½–⅔ cup warm water
lime wedges, to garnish

FOR THE SALSA
1 red onion, finely chopped
1 fresh red chilli, seeded and finely chopped
2 tbsp chopped fresh dill or coriander
½ cucumber, peeled and chopped
6 oz alfalfa sprouts

FOR THE SAUCE
1 large ripe avocado, peeled and pitted
juice of 1 lime
2 tbsp soft goat cheese
pinch of paprika

avocado

goat cheese

red chilli

cucumber

dill

alfalfa sprouts

COOK'S TIP
When peeling the avocado be sure to scrape off the bright green flesh from immediately under the skin as this gives the sauce its vivid green color.

1 Mix all the salsa ingredients together in a bowl and set aside.

2 To make the sauce, place the avocado, lime juice and goat cheese in a food processor or blender and blend until smooth. Place in a bowl and cover with plastic wrap. Dust with paprika just before serving.

3 To make the tortillas, place the flour and salt in a food processor, add the oil and blend. Gradually add the water (the amount will vary depending on the type of flour). Stop adding water when a stiff dough has formed. Turn out onto a floured board and knead until smooth. Cover with a damp cloth.

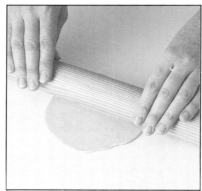

4 Divide the mixture into 8 pieces. Knead each piece for a couple of minutes and form into a ball. Flatten and roll out each ball to a 9 in circle.

5 Heat an ungreased cast-iron pan. Cook 1 tortilla at a time for about 30 seconds on each side. Place the cooked tortillas in a clean dish-towel and repeat until you have 8 tortillas.

6 To serve, spread each tortilla with a spoonful of avocado sauce, top with salsa and roll up. Garnish with lime wedges.

Pear and Pecan Salad with Blue Cheese Dressing

Toasted pecans have a special affinity for crisp white pears. Their robust flavors combine especially well with a rich blue cheese dressing and make this a salad to remember.

Serves 4

INGREDIENTS
½ cup shelled pecans, roughly chopped
3 crisp pears
6 oz young spinach, stems removed
1 escarole or Boston lettuce
1 radicchio
2 tbsp Blue Cheese and Chive Dressing
salt and pepper
crusty bread, to serve

1 Toast the pecans under a moderate broiler to bring out their flavor.

2 Cut the pears into even slices, leaving the skin intact, and discarding the cores.

3 Wash the salad leaves and spin dry. Add the pears together with the toasted pecans, then toss with the dressing. Distribute between 4 large plates and season with salt and pepper. Serve with warm crusty bread.

escarole

pears

pecans

radicchio

spinach

Melon and Prosciutto Salad with Strawberry Salsa

Sections of cool fragrant melon wrapped with slices of air-dried ham make a delicious salad starter. If strawberries are in season, serve with a savory-sweet strawberry salsa and watch it disappear.

Serves 4

INGREDIENTS
1 large melon, cantaloupe, Spanish or
  charentais
6 oz prosciutto, thinly sliced

SALSA
½ lb strawberries
1 tsp superfine sugar
2 tbsp peanut or sunflower oil
1 tbsp orange juice
½ tsp finely grated orange zest
½ tsp finely grated fresh ginger
salt and black pepper

1 Halve the melon and take the seeds out with a spoon. Cut the rind away with a paring knife, then slice the melon thickly. Chill until ready to serve.

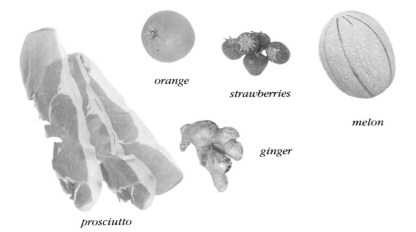

orange

strawberries

ginger

melon

prosciutto

2 To make the salsa, hull the strawberries and cut them into large dice. Place in a small mixing bowl with the sugar and crush lightly to release the juices. Add the oil, orange juice, zest, and ginger. Season with salt and a generous twist of black pepper.

3 Arrange the melon on a serving plate, lay the ham over the top, and serve with a bowl of salsa.

Pasta with Shrimp and Feta Cheese

This dish combines the richness of fresh shrimp with the tartness of feta cheese. Goat cheese could be used as an alternative.

Serves 4

INGREDIENTS
1 lb medium raw shrimp
6 scallions
4 tbsp butter
½ lb feta cheese
salt and pepper
small bunch fresh chives
1 lb penne, garganelle, or rigatoni

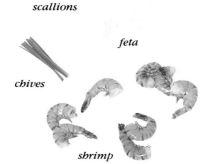

penne

scallions

feta

chives

shrimp

1 Remove the heads from the shrimp by twisting and pulling off. Peel the shrimp and discard the shells. Chop the scallions.

2 Melt the butter in a skillet and stir in the shrimp. When they turn pink, add the scallions and cook gently for 1 minute.

3 Cut the feta into ½ in cubes.

4 Stir the feta cheese into the shrimp mixture, and season with plenty of black pepper.

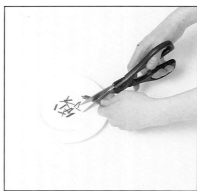

5 Cut the chives into 1 in lengths and stir half into the shrimp.

6 Cook the pasta in plenty of boiling salted water according to the manufacturer's instructions. Drain well, pile into a warmed serving dish, and top with the sauce. Scatter with the remaining chives and serve.

Chicken Goujons

Serve as a first course for eight people or as a filling main course for four. Delicious served with new potatoes and salad.

Serves 8

INGREDIENTS
4 boned and skinned chicken breasts
3 cups fresh bread crumbs
1 tsp ground coriander
2 tsp ground paprika
½ tsp ground cumin
3 tbsp all-purpose flour
2 eggs, beaten
oil, for deep-frying
salt and freshly ground black pepper
lemon slices, to garnish
sprigs of fresh coriander, to garnish

FOR THE DIP
1¼ cups plain yogurt
2 tbsp lemon juice
4 tbsp chopped fresh coriander
4 tbsp chopped fresh parsley

bread crumbs

flour

eggs

lemon

yogurt

coriander

parsley

chicken breast

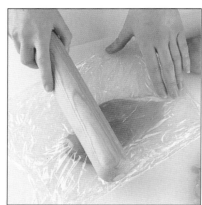

1 Divide the chicken breasts into two natural fillets. Place them between two sheets of plastic wrap and, using a rolling pin, flatten each one to a thickness of about ¼ in.

2 Cut into 1 in strips diagonally across the fillets.

3 Mix the bread crumbs with the spices and seasoning. Toss the chicken fillet pieces (goujons) into the flour, keeping them separate.

4 Dip the fillets into the beaten egg and then coat in the bread crumb mixture.

5 Thoroughly mix all the ingredients for the dip together, and season to taste. Chill until required.

6 Heat the oil in a heavy-based pan. It is ready for deep-frying when a cube of bread tossed into the oil sizzles on the surface. Fry the goujons in batches until golden and crisp. Drain on paper towels and keep warm in the oven until all the chicken has been fried. Garnish with lemon slices and sprigs of fresh coriander.

Fillets of Pink Trout with Tarragon Cream Sauce

If you do not like the idea of cooking and serving trout on the bone, ask your fishmonger to fillet and skin the fish. Serve two fillets per person.

VARIATION
This recipe can also be made with salmon fillets and the dry sherry may be substituted with white wine.

Serves 4

INGREDIENTS
2 tbsp butter
4 fresh trout, filleted and skinned
salt and freshly ground black pepper
new potatoes, to serve
wax beans, to serve

FOR THE CREAM SAUCE
2 large scallions, white part only, chopped
½ cucumber, peeled, deseeded and cut into short sticks
1 tsp cornstarch
⅔ cup light cream
¼ cup dry sherry
2 tbsp chopped fresh tarragon
1 tomato, chopped and deseeded

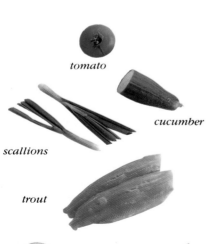

tomato

cucumber

scallions

trout

cream   *tarragon*

1 Melt the butter in a large frying pan, season the fillets and cook for 6 minutes, turning once. Transfer to a plate, cover and keep warm.

2 To make the sauce, add the scallions and cucumber to the pan, and cook over a gentle heat, stirring occasionally, until soft but not colored.

3 Remove the pan from the heat and stir in the cornstarch.

4 Return to the heat and pour in the cream and sherry. Simmer to thicken, stirring continuously.

5 Add the chopped tarragon and tomato, and season to taste.

6 Spoon the sauce over the fillets and serve with buttered new potatoes and wax beans.

Shrimp Salad with Curry Dressing

Curry spices add an unexpected twist to this salad. Warm flavors combine especially well with sweet shrimp and grated apple.

Serves 4

INGREDIENTS
1 ripe tomato
½ iceberg lettuce, shredded
1 small onion
1 small bunch fresh cilantro
1 tbsp lemon juice
salt
1 lb cooked peeled shrimp
1 apple, peeled

DRESSING
5 tbsp mayonnaise
1 tsp mild curry paste
1 tbsp tomato ketchup

TO DECORATE
8 whole shrimp
8 lemon wedges
4 sprigs fresh cilantro

2 Finely shred the lettuce, onion, and cilantro. Add the tomato, toss with lemon juice, and season with salt.

3 To make the dressing, combine the mayonnaise, curry paste, and tomato ketchup in a small bowl. Add 2 tbsp water to thin the dressing and season to taste with salt.

1 To peel the tomato, pierce the skin with a knife and immerse in boiling water for 20 seconds. Drain and cool under running water. Peel off the skin. Halve the tomato, push the seeds out with your thumb, and discard them. Cut the flesh into a large dice.

4 Combine the shrimp with the dressing. Quarter and core the apple, and grate into the mixture.

tomato   *apple*

cilantro

lemon   *onion*

shrimp

COOK'S TIP

Fresh cilantro is inclined to wilt if kept out of water. Keep it in a jar of water in the refrigerator covered with a plastic bag and it will stay fresh for several days.

5 Distribute the shredded lettuce mixture between 4 plates or bowls. Pile the shrimp mixture in the center of each and decorate with 2 whole shrimp, 2 lemon wedges, and a sprig of cilantro.

Fillets of Striped Bass Baked with Thyme and Garlic

Quick cooking is the essence of this dish. Use the freshest garlic available and half the amount of dried thyme if fresh is not available.

Serves 4

INGREDIENTS
1 shallot, finely chopped
2 garlic cloves, thinly sliced
4 sprigs fresh thyme, plus extra to
    garnish
4 × 6 oz striped bass fillets
grated rind and juice of 1 lemon, plus
    extra juice for drizzling
2 tbsp extra virgin olive oil
salt and freshly ground black pepper

garlic

lemon

shallot

striped bass
fillet

thyme

1 Preheat the oven to 350°F. Lay the bass fillets into the base of a large roasting tin. Scatter the shallot, garlic cloves and thyme on top.

2 Season well with salt and pepper.

3 Drizzle over the lemon juice and oil. Bake for about 15 minutes in the pre-heated oven. Serve scattered with finely grated lemon rind and garnished with thyme sprigs.

VARIATION
If striped bass is not available you can use cod or haddock fillets for this recipe. You can also use a mixture of fresh herbs rather than just thyme.

Stuffed Sardines

This Middle Eastern-inspired dish doesn't take a lot of preparation and is a meal in itself. Just serve with a crisp green salad tossed in a fresh lemon vinaigrette to make it complete.

Serves 4

INGREDIENTS
2 lb fresh sardines
2 tbsp olive oil
½ cup wholewheat bread
  crumbs
¼ cup raisins
½ cup pine nuts
2 oz canned anchovy fillets,
  drained
4 tbsp chopped fresh parsley
1 onion, finely chopped
salt and freshly ground black pepper
lemon wedges, to garnish

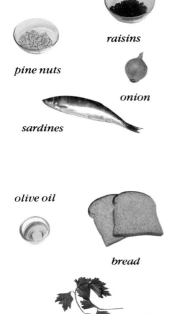

raisins

pine nuts

onion

sardines

olive oil

bread

parsley

1 Preheat the oven to 400°F. Gut the sardines and wipe out thoroughly with paper towels. Heat the oil in a frying pan and fry the bread crumbs until golden.

2 Add the raisins, pine nuts, anchovies, parsley, onion and seasoning and mix well.

3 Stuff each sardine with the mixture. Close the fish firmly and place, closely packed together in an ovenproof dish.

4 Scatter any remaining filling over the sardines and drizzle over the remaining olive oil. Bake for 30 minutes in the preheated oven and serve garnished with fresh lemon wedges.

Salmon with Spicy Pesto

This is a great way to serve boned salmon steaks as a solid piece of fish. It's also cheaper than buying fillet if you have to pay for the fishmonger boning it. The pesto is unusual because it uses sunflower kernels and chili as its flavoring rather than the classic basil and pine nuts.

Serves 4

INGREDIENTS
4 × ½ lb salmon steaks
2 tbsp sunflower oil
finely grated rind and juice of 1 lime
salt and freshly ground black pepper

For the pesto
6 mild fresh red chilies
2 garlic cloves
2 tbsp pumpkin or sunflower
   seeds
finely grated rind and juice of 1 lime
5 tbsp olive oil

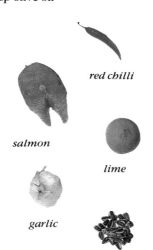

red chilli

salmon

lime

garlic

pumpkin seeds

1 Insert a very sharp knife closely to the top of the bone. Working closely to the bone, cut your way to the end of the steak so one side of the steak has been released and one side is still attached. Repeat with the other side. Pull out any extra visible bones with a pair of tweezers.

2 Sprinkle a little salt on the surface and take hold of the end of the salmon piece skin-side down. Insert a small sharp knife under the skin and, working away from you, cut off the skin keeping as close to the skin as possible. Repeat with the other pieces of fish.

3 Wrap each piece of fish into a circle, with the thinner end wrapped around the fatter end. Secure tightly with a length of string.

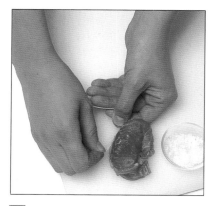

4 Rub the sunflower oil into the boneless fish rounds. Add the lime juice and rind and marinate in the refrigerator for 2 hours.

5 For the pesto, de-seed the chilies, and place them together with the garlic cloves, pumpkin seeds, lime juice, rind and seasoning into a food processor fitted with a metal blade. Process until well mixed. Pour the olive oil gradually over the moving blades until the sauce has thickened and emulsified. Drain the salmon from its marinade. Broil the fish steaks for 5 minutes either side and serve with the spicy pesto.

Fish Curry

Any mixture of white fish works well with this fresh curry. Serve with warm naan bread to mop up the delicious juices.

Serves 4

INGREDIENTS
1½ lb white boneless fish such as halibut, cod, pollock or monkfish
juice of ½ lime
2 tsp cider vinegar
4 cups grated fresh coconut
1 in piece of ginger root, peeled and grated
6 garlic cloves
1 lb tomatoes, chopped
3 tbsp sunflower oil
¾ lb onions, roughly chopped
20 curry leaves
1 tsp ground coriander
½ tsp ground turmeric
2 tsp ground chili
½ tsp fenugreek seeds
½ tsp cumin seeds
salt and freshly ground black pepper
banana leaves, to serve
lime slices, to garnish

lime

cider vinegar

ginger

garlic

onion

white fish

tomato

fresh coconut

1 Marinate the fish in lime juice, vinegar and a pinch of salt for 30 minutes.

2 In a food processor fitted with a metal blade, process the grated coconut, ginger, garlic cloves and tomatoes to make a paste.

3 Heat the oil in a frying pan, add the onions and cook until golden brown, then add the curry leaves.

4 Add the coriander, turmeric and chili and stir-fry for 1 minute.

5 Add the coconut paste and cook for 3–4 minutes, constantly stirring. Pour in 1¼ cups water, bring to the boil, and simmer for 4 minutes.

6 Pound the fenugreek and cumin seeds together in a pestle and mortar. Lay the fish on top of the simmering sauce, sprinkle over the fenugreek mixture and cook for 15 minutes or until the fish is tender. Serve on banana leaves and garnish with lime slices.

Halibut with Fresh Tomato and Basil Salsa

Take care when cooking this dish as the fish tends to break up very easily, especially as the skin has been removed. Season well to bring out the delicate flavor of the halibut and the fresh taste of the sauce.

Serves 4

INGREDIENTS

For the salsa
1 medium tomato, roughly chopped
¼ red onion, finely chopped
1 small jalapeño pepper
2 tbsp balsamic vinegar
10 large fresh basil leaves
1 tbsp olive oil
salt and freshly ground black pepper

For the fish
4 × 6 oz halibut fillets
3 tbsp olive oil

tomato

jalapeño pepper

halibut fillet

basil

red onion

1 In a bowl mix together the tomato, red onion, jalapeño pepper and balsamic vinegar.

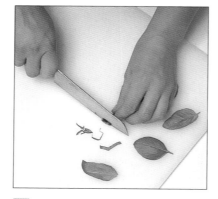

2 Slice the basil leaves finely.

3 Stir the basil and the olive oil into the tomato mixture. Season to taste. Cover and leave to marinate for at least 3 hours.

4 For the fish, rub the halibut fillets with olive oil and seasoning. Heat a broiler or barbecue and cook for about 4 minutes either side depending on the thickness of each fillet. Baste with olive oil as necessary. Serve with the salsa.

Cod and Spinach Parcels

The best way to serve this dish is to slice each parcel into about four and reveal the meaty large flakes of white fish. Drizzle the sauce over the slices.

Serves 4

INGREDIENTS
4 × 6 oz pieces of thick cod fillet,
    skinned
8 oz large spinach leaves
½ tsp freshly ground nutmeg
3 tbsp white wine
salt and freshly ground black pepper

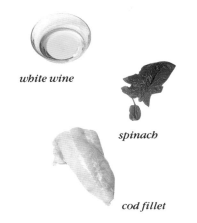

white wine

spinach

cod fillet

1 Preheat the oven to 350°F. Season the fish well with salt and freshly ground black pepper.

2 Blanch the spinach leaves in boiling water for a minute and refresh under cold water.

3 Pat the spinach leaves dry on absorbent paper towels.

4 Wrap the spinach around each fish fillet. Sprinkle with nutmeg. Place in a roasting tin, pour over the wine and poach for 15 minutes. Slice and serve hot.

San Francisco Salad

California is a salad maker's paradise and is renowned for the healthiness of its produce. San Francisco has become the salad capital of California, although this recipe is based on a salad served at the Chez Panisse restaurant in Berkeley.

Serves 4

INGREDIENTS
2 lb langoustines, or jumbo shrimp
salt and cayenne pepper
2 oz bulb fennel, sliced
2 ripe medium tomatoes, quartered, and 4 small tomatoes
2 tbsp olive oil, plus extra for tossing the salad leaves
4 tbsp brandy
⅔ cup dry white wine
7 fl oz can lobster or crab bisque
2 tbsp chopped fresh tarragon
3 tbsp heavy cream
8 oz green beans, trimmed and stringed
2 oranges
6 oz lamb's lettuce
¼ lb arugula
½ frisée lettuce

frisée lettuce

langoustines

tomatoes   *fennel*   *orange*

lamb's lettuce

arugula

1 Bring a large saucepan of salted water to a boil, add the langoustines (or shrimp), and simmer for 10 minutes. Refresh under cold running water.

2 Preheat the oven to 425°F. Twist the tails from all but 4 of the langoustines (or peel and devein the shrimp): reserve these to garnish the dish. Peel the outer shell from the tail. Put the tail peelings, carapace and claws in a roasting pan with the fennel and tomatoes. Toss with 2 tbsp oil and roast near the top of the oven for 20 minutes.

3 Remove the roasting pan from the oven and place it over a moderate heat on top of the stove. Add the brandy and ignite to release the flavor of the alcohol. Add the wine and simmer briefly.

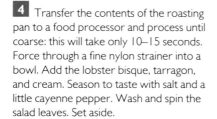

4 Transfer the contents of the roasting pan to a food processor and process until coarse: this will take only 10–15 seconds. Force through a fine nylon strainer into a bowl. Add the lobster bisque, tarragon, and cream. Season to taste with salt and a little cayenne pepper. Wash and spin the salad leaves. Set aside.

5 Bring a saucepan of salted water to a boil and cook the beans for 6 minutes. Drain and cool under running water. To segment the oranges, cut the peel from the top and bottom, and then from the sides, with a serrated knife. Loosen the segments by cutting between the membranes and the flesh.

6 Toss the lettuce with olive oil and distribute between 4 serving plates. Fold the langoustine or shrimp into the dressing and distribute between the plates. Add the beans, oranges, and small tomatoes, decorate each with a whole langoustine (or shrimp) and serve warm.

Vietnamese Stuffed Squid

The smaller the squid the sweeter the dish will taste. Be very careful not to overcook the flesh as it becomes tough very quickly.

Serves 4

INGREDIENTS

2 lb (appx. 8 medium-sized) squid, cleaned
2 oz cellophane noodles
2 tbsp peanut oil
2 scallions, finely chopped
8 shiitake mushrooms, halved if large
9 oz ground pork
1 garlic clove, chopped
2 tbsp Thai fish sauce
1 tsp sugar
1 tbsp finely chopped cilantro
1 tsp lemon juice
salt and freshly ground pepper

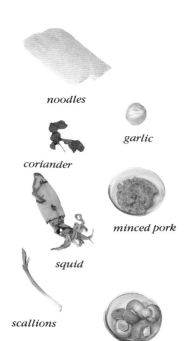

noodles

garlic

coriander

minced pork

squid

scallions

shiitake mushrooms

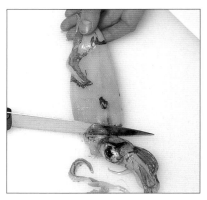

1 Preheat the oven to 400°F. Clean the squid and remove any excess membrane and tentacles.

2 Put the noodles into a saucepan of boiling water. Remove the pan from the heat and soak the noodles for 20 minutes.

3 Heat 1 tbsp of the oil in a wok and stir-fry the scallions, mushrooms, pork and garlic for 4 minutes until the meat is golden.

4 Add the noodles, fish sauce, sugar, seasoning, cilantro and lemon juice.

5 Stuff the squid two-thirds full with the mixture and secure with toothsticks or satay sticks. Drizzle over the remaining oil, prick the squid twice and bake in the preheated oven for 10 minutes. Serve hot.

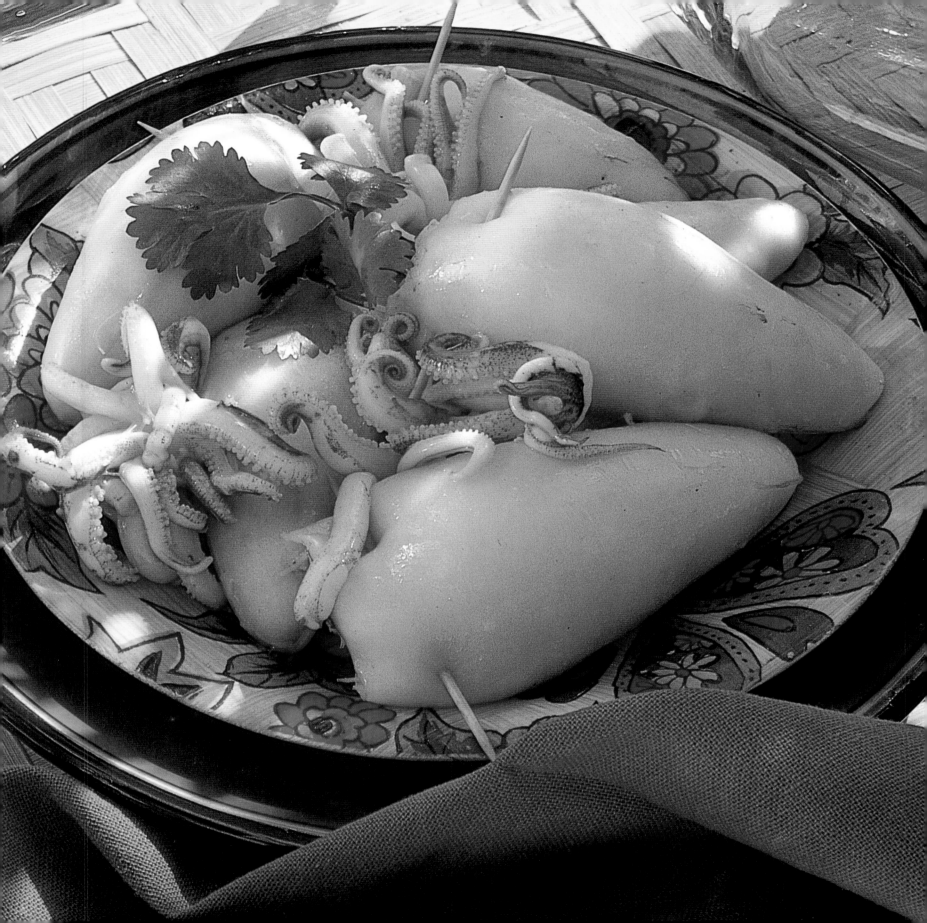

Classic Whole Salmon

Serving a boneless whole salmon is a delight. Take care when cooking the fish. If you own a fish poacher the method is slightly different. Cover with water, a dash of white wine, add a bay leaf, sliced lemon and black peppercorns and bring to a boil for 6 minutes. Leave to cool completely in the water until cold. Drain, pat dry, and continue as instructed in the recipe.

Serves 8

INGREDIENTS
1 whole salmon
1¼ cups water
⅔ cup white wine
3 bay leaves
1 lemon, sliced
12 black peppercorns
2 cucumbers; thinly sliced
mixed fresh herbs such as parsley, chervil and chives, to garnish
mayonnaise

cucumber

salmon

lemon

bay leaves

1 Preheat the oven to 350°F. Clean the inside of the salmon making sure all the gut has been removed and the inside cavity has been well wiped out with paper towels. Cut the tail into a neat "V" shape with a sharp pair of scissors. Place the fish on a large piece of heavy aluminum foil. Lay the bay leaves, sliced lemon and black peppercorns inside the cavity. Wrap the foil around and up the sides, and pour over the water and wine. Seal the parcel and place in a large roasting pan.

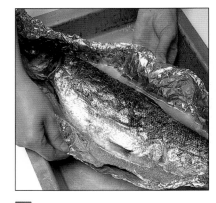

2 Bake in the preheated oven, allowing 15 minutes per pound plus 15 minutes extra. Remove from the oven, open up the parcel and leave to cool. Don't leave to chill overnight as the skin will be impossible to remove the next day.

3 Cut off the head and tail, reserving them if you want them to display the fish later. Turn the fish upside-down onto a board so the flattest side is uppermost. Carefully peel off the base foil and the skin. Using a sharp knife, scrap away any excess brown flesh from the pink salmon flesh.

4 Make an incision down the back fillet, drawing the flesh away from the central bone. Take one fillet and place on the serving dish. Remove the second fillet and place it beside the first to form the base of the fish.

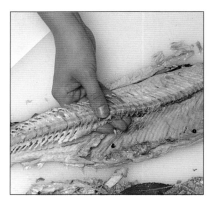

5 Remove the central back bone from the fish.

6 Place the other half of the fish with the skin still intact, flesh-side down on top of the base fish. Peel off the upper skin and any brown bits. Replace the head and tail if required. Using the cucumber slices, lay them on top of the fish working from the tail end until all the flesh is covered and the cucumber resembles scales. Garnish the plate with large bunches of fresh herbs and serve with mayonnaise.

Salmon Coulibiac

A complicated Russian dish that takes a lot of preparation, but is well worth it. Traditionally sturgeon is used but as this is difficult to get hold of salmon may be substituted. As a special treat serve with shots of vodka for an authentic Russian flavor.

Serves 8

INGREDIENTS
For the blinis
2 eggs, separated
3 cups milk
2 cups flour
1 ½ cups butter, melted
½ tsp salt
½ tsp sugar

For the filling
4 tbsp butter
¾ lb mushrooms, sliced
½ cup white wine
juice of ½ lemon
½ lb salmon fillet, skinned
½ cup long grain rice
1 large onion, chopped
2 tbsp chopped fresh dill
4 hard-boiled eggs, sliced

1 lb puff pastry
salt and freshly ground black pepper
lemon wedges, to garnish
fresh dill sprigs, to garnish

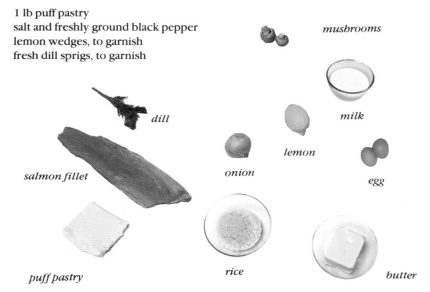

dill

salmon fillet

onion

lemon

mushrooms

milk

egg

rice

butter

puff pastry

1 For the blinis, whisk the egg yolks together and add the milk. Gradually beat in the flour, 11 ½ oz of the melted butter, salt and sugar until smooth. Leave to stand for 30 minutes.

2 Whisk the egg whites until they just form stiff peaks, then fold into the batter. Heat the remaining butter in a heavy-based frying pan and add about 3 tbsp of the batter. Turn and cook until golden. Repeat until all the mixture has been used up, brushing on a little melted butter when stacking the pancakes. When they are cool, cut into long rectangles and cover until ready to use.

3 For the filling, melt the butter in a large frying pan and add the mushrooms. Cook for 3 minutes. Add 60 ml/4 tbsp of the wine and boil for 2 minutes, then simmer for a further 5 minutes. Add the remaining wine and lemon juice.

4 Place the salmon on top of the cooked mushrooms, cover with foil, and gently steam for 8–10 minutes until just cooked. Remove the salmon from the pan and set aside.

5 Set aside the mushrooms and pour the cooking liquid into a large clean pan. Add the rice and cook for 10–15 minutes until tender adding more wine if necessary. Remove from the heat and stir in the dill and seasoning. Melt the remaining butter and fry the onion until brown. Set aside.

6 Grease a large baking tray. Flour a clean dish towel, then roll the pastry onto it into a rectangle 12 × 20 in in diameter. Leaving 1 ¼ in at the top ends of the pastry, place half the pancakes in a strip up the middle of the dough. Top with half the rice mixture, half the onion, half the hard-boiled egg, and half the mushrooms. Place all the salmon fillets on top of the mushrooms and press down gently. Continue the layering process in reverse.

7 Take the 1 ¼ in ends and wrap gently over the filling and then fold over the long ends. Brush with beaten egg to seal, and transfer to the baking sheet rolling it off the dish towel facing seam-side down. Chill for an hour. Preheat the oven to 425°F. Cut four small slits in the top and bake for 10 minutes. Turn the oven down to 375°F and bake for 30 minutes until golden brown. Serve sliced, garnished with lemon wedges and fresh dill sprigs.

Tuscan Tuna and Beans

A great kitchen-cupboard dish, which is especially good for children as there are no bones.

Serves 4

INGREDIENTS

1 red onion, finely chopped
2 tbsp smooth French mustard
1¼ cups olive oil
4 tbsp white wine vinegar
2 tbsp chopped fresh parsley, plus
    extra to garnish
2 tbsp chopped fresh chives
2 tbsp chopped fresh tarragon or
    chervil
1 × 14 oz can navy beans
1 × 14 oz can kidney beans
8 oz canned tuna in oil, drained and
    lightly flaked

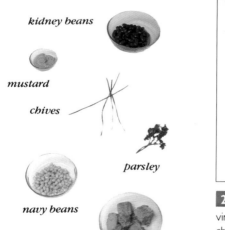

kidney beans

mustard

chives

parsley

navy beans

tuna

red onion

tarragon

1 Chop the onion finely.

2 In a small bowl, beat the mustard, oil, vinegar, parsley, chives and tarragon or chervil together.

3 Rinse and drain the canned beans.

4 Mix the red onion, beans and dressing together thoroughly, toss well and serve.

Broiled Porgy with Fennel, Mustard and Orange

Porgy is a revelation to anyone unfamiliar with its creamy rich flavor. The fish has a firm white flesh that partners well with a rich butter sauce, sharpened here with a dash of frozen orange juice concentrate.

Serves 2

INGREDIENTS
2 baking potatoes
2 × 12 oz porgies, scaled and
    gutted
2 tsp Dijon mustard
1 tsp fennel seeds
2 tbsp olive oil
2 oz watercress
6 oz mixed lettuce leaves, such as
    curly endive or frisée

FOR THE SAUCE
2 tbsp frozen orange juice
    concentrate
¾ cup unsalted butter,
    diced
salt and cayenne pepper

Dijon mustard

orange juice

cayenne pepper

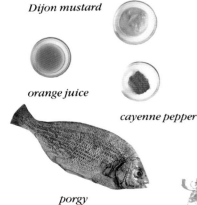
porgy

lettuce

COOK'S TIP

For speedy baked potatoes, microwave small potatoes on 100% high power for 8 minutes, then crisp in a hot oven preheated to 400°F for a further 10 minutes. Split, butter and serve hot.

1 Cook the potatoes according to the tip at the beginning of this recipe. Preheat a moderate broiler. Slash the porgies four times on either side. Combine the mustard and fennel seeds, then spread over both sides of the fish. Moisten with oil and broil for 12 minutes, turning once.

2 Place the orange juice concentrate in a bowl and heat over 1 in of boiling water. Remove the pan from the stove, and gradually whisk the butter until creamy. Season, cover and set aside.

3 Moisten the watercress and lettuce leaves with the remaining olive oil, arrange the fish on two large plates and put the leaves to one side. Spoon over the sauce and serve with the potatoes.

Barbecued Salmon with Red Onion Marmalade

Salmon barbecues well but make sure it is at least 2.5 cm/1 in thick to make it easy to turn when cooking. The red onion marmalade is rich and delicious. Substitute a tablespoon of pureed blackcurrants for the blackcurrant liqueur if you like.

Serves 4

INGREDIENTS
4 salmon steaks, cut 1 in thick, no
 thinner
2 tbsp olive oil
salt and freshly ground black pepper

For the red onion marmalade
5 medium red onions, peeled
4 tbsp butter
¾ cup red wine vinegar
¼ cup blackcurrant liqueur
¼ cup grenadine
¼ cup red wine

red wine

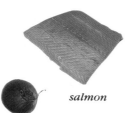

salmon

red onion

butter

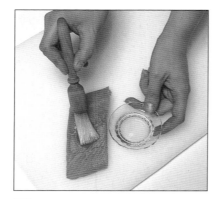

1 Rub the olive oil into the fish flesh.

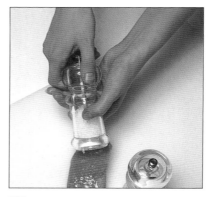

2 Season the fish well with salt and pepper.

3 Finely slice the onions.

4 Melt the butter in a large heavy-based saucepan and add the onions. Sauté for 5 minutes.

5 Stir in the vinegar, cassis, grenadine and wine and continue to cook until the liquid has reduced. It should take about 10 minutes until the liquid has almost entirely evaporated and the onions are glazed. Season well.

6 Brush the fish with a little more oil, and barbecue or broil for 4 minutes on either side.

Poached Skate and Brown Butter

Skate is one of those fish which actually improves after storing for a couple of days in the refrigerator. The capers in this dish can be omitted, leaving the simple burnt butter flavor standing on its own.

Serves 4

INGREDIENTS
4½ cups water
1 carrot, sliced
1 small onion, sliced
bouquet garni
6 peppercorns
½ cup white wine vinegar
1 tsp salt
2 lb skate wings divided
    into 4

For the blackened butter
½ cup butter
2 tbsp drained capers

peppercorns

onion

carrot

butter

skate wings

bouquet garni

1 Place the water, carrot, onion, bouquet garni, peppercorns and ½ cup white wine vinegar and salt into a large, heavy-based saucepan. Bring to a boil and simmer uncovered for 20 minutes. Strain the liquid and discard the vegetables, reserving the liquid.

2 Poach the skate wings in the liquid for about 10 minutes. Drain and keep warm.

3 Meanwhile, make the brown butter. Heat the butter in a pan until it turns brown. Remove from the heat and stir in the capers.

4 Pour the butter over the skate and deglaze the pan with the remaining vinegar and pour on top.

Thick Cod Fillet with Fresh Mixed-herb Crust

Mixed fresh herbs make this a delicious crust. Season well and serve with large lemon wedges.

Serves 4

INGREDIENTS
2 tbsp butter
1 tbsp fresh chervil
1 tbsp fresh parsley
1 tbsp fresh chives
3 cups wholewheat bread
    crumbs
4 × 8 oz thickly cut cod fillets,
    skinned
1 tbsp olive oil
lemon wedges, to garnish
salt and freshly ground black pepper

chives
butter
bread crumbs
parsley
cod fillets
chervil
lemon

1 Preheat the oven to 400°F. Melt the butter and chop the fresh herbs finely.

2 Mix the butter with the bread crumbs, herbs and seasoning.

3 Press a quarter of the mixture on top of each fillet. Place on a baking sheet and drizzle over the olive oil. Bake in the preheated oven for 15 minutes until the fish flesh is firm and the top turns golden. Serve garnished with lemon wedges.

Turkey Tonnato

This low fat version of the Italian dish 'vitello tonnato' is garnished with fine strips of red pepper instead of the traditional anchovy fillets.

Serves 4

INGREDIENTS
1 lb turkey fillets
1 small onion, sliced
1 bay leaf
4 black peppercorns
1½ cups fresh chicken stock
7 oz can tuna in water, drained
5 tbsp reduced calorie mayonnaise
2 tbsp lemon juice
2 red bell peppers, seeded and
   thinly sliced
about 25 capers, drained
pinch of salt
mixed salad and tomatoes, to serve

tuna

lemon

bay leaf

onion

capers

mayonnaise

pepper

turkey fillet

stock

1 Put the turkey fillets in a single layer in a large, heavy-based saucepan. Add the onion, bay leaf, peppercorns and stock. Bring to a boil and reduce the heat. Cover and simmer for 12 minutes, or until tender.

2 Turn off the heat and leave the turkey to cool in the stock, then remove with a slotted spoon. Slice thickly and arrange on a serving plate.

3 Boil the stock until reduced to about 5 tbsp. Strain and leave to cool.

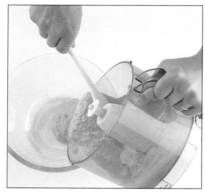

4 Put the tuna, mayonnaise, lemon juice, 3 tbsp of the reduced stock and salt into a blender or food processor and purée until smooth.

5 Stir in enough of the remaining stock to reduce the sauce to the thickness of heavy cream. Spoon over the turkey.

6 Arrange the strips of red pepper in a lattice pattern over the turkey. Put a caper in the center of each square. Chill in the refrigerator for 1 hour and serve with a fresh mixed salad and tomatoes.

Poor Boy Steak Salad

'Poor Boy' started life in the Italian Creole community of New Orleans when the poor survived on sandwiches filled with leftover scraps. Times have improved since then, and today the 'Poor Boy' sandwich is commonly filled with tender beef strips and other goodies. This is a salad version of 'Poor Boy'.

Serves 4

INGREDIENTS
4 sirloin or rump steaks, each
    weighing 6 oz
1 escarole lettuce
1 bunch watercress
4 tomatoes, quartered
4 large dill pickles, sliced
4 scallions, sliced
4 canned artichoke hearts, halved
6 oz button mushrooms, sliced
12 green olives
½ cup French Dressing
salt and black pepper

1 Season the steaks with black pepper. Cook the steaks under a moderate broiler for 6–8 minutes, turning once, until medium-rare. Cover and leave to rest in a warm place.

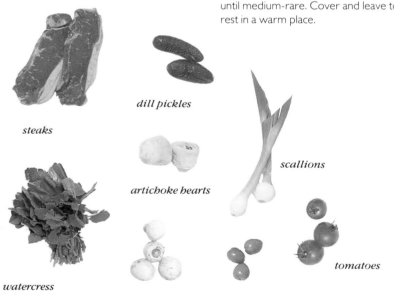

steaks

dill pickles

artichoke hearts

scallions

watercress

mushrooms

olives

tomatoes

2 Wash the salad leaves and spin dry. Combine with the remainder of the ingredients (except the steak) and toss with the French Dressing.

3 Divide the salad between 4 plates. Slice each steak diagonally and position over the salad. Season with salt and serve.

Waldorf Ham Salad

Waldorf salad first appeared at the Waldorf Astoria Hotel, New York, in the 1890s. Originally it consisted of apples, celery, and mayonnaise. It was commonly served with duck, ham, and goose. This modern-day version often includes meat and is something of a meal in itself.

Serves 4

INGREDIENTS
3 apples, peeled
1 tbsp lemon juice
2 slices cooked ham, each weighing
   6 oz
3 stalks celery
⅔ cup mayonnaise
1 escarole or Batavia lettuce
1 small radicchio, finely shredded
½ bunch watercress
3 tbsp walnut oil or olive oil
½ cup walnut pieces, toasted
salt and pepper

2 Add the mayonnaise to the apples, ham, and celery and mix well.

3 Wash and spin the salad leaves. Shred the leaves finely, then toss with walnut oil. Distribute the leaves between 4 plates. Pile the mayonnaise mixture in the center, scatter with toasted walnuts, season, and serve.

1 Core, slice, and shred the apples finely. Moisten with lemon juice to keep them white. Cut the ham into 2 in strips, then cut the celery into similar-sized pieces, and combine in a bowl.

apple

watercress

celery

radicchio

walnuts

escarole

Rockburger Salad with Sesame Croutons

This salad plays on the ingredients that make up the all-American hamburger in a sesame bun. Inside the burger is a special layer of Roquefort, a blue ewe's-milk cheese from France.

COOK'S TIP

If you're planning ahead, it's a good idea to freeze the filled burgers between pieces of waxed paper. They will keep in the freezer for up to 8 weeks.

Serves 4

INGREDIENTS
2 lb lean ground beef
1 egg
1 medium onion, finely chopped
2 tsp French mustard
½ tsp celery salt
black pepper
4 oz Roquefort or other blue cheese
1 large sesame seed bread loaf
3 tbsp olive oil, preferably Spanish
1 small iceberg lettuce
2 oz arugula or watercress
½ cup French Dressing
4 ripe tomatoes, quartered
4 large scallions, sliced

1 Place the ground beef, egg, onion, mustard, celery salt, and pepper in a mixing bowl. Combine thoroughly. Divide the mixture into 16 portions, each weighing about 2 oz.

2 Flatten the pieces between 2 sheets of plastic wrap or waxed paper to form 5 in rounds.

3 Place ½ oz of the cheese on 8 of the thin burgers. Sandwich with the remainder and press the edges firmly. Store between pieces of plastic wrap or waxed paper and chill until ready to cook.

arugula

iceberg lettuce

egg

ground beef

blue cheese

sesame seed bread

4 To make the sesame croutons, preheat the broiler to a moderate temperature. Remove the sesame crust from the bread, then cut the crust into short fingers. Brush with olive oil and toast evenly for 10–15 minutes.

5 Season the burgers and broil for 10 minutes, turning once.

6 Wash the salad leaves and spin dry. Toss with the dressing, then distribute between 4 large plates. Place 2 of the rockburgers in the center of each plate and arrange the tomatoes, scallions, and sesame croutons around the edge.

Frankfurter Salad with Mustard and Caraway Dressing

A last-minute salad you can throw together using ingredients from the pantry.

Serves 4

INGREDIENTS
1½ lb small new potatoes, scrubbed or scraped
2 eggs
12 oz frankfurters
1 butterhead or Batavia lettuce
½ lb young spinach, stems removed

DRESSING
salt and pepper
3 tbsp safflower oil
2 tbsp olive oil, preferably Spanish
1 tbsp white-wine vinegar
2 tsp mustard
1 tsp caraway seeds, crushed

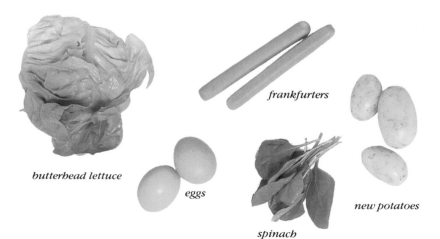

1 Bring the potatoes to a boil in salted water and simmer for 20 minutes. Drain, cover, and keep warm. Boil the eggs for 12 minutes. Refresh in cold water, shell, and cut into quarters.

2 Score the frankfurter skins cork-screw fashion with a small knife, then cover with boiling water and simmer for about 5 minutes to heat through. Drain well, cover, and keep warm.

butterhead lettuce

eggs

frankfurters

spinach

new potatoes

3 Combine the dressing ingredients in a screw-top jar and shake.

4 Wash and spin the salad leaves, toss with half of the dressing, and distribute between 4 large plates.

5 Toss the potatoes and frankfurters with the remainder of the dressing, and scatter over the salad.

6 Finish with sections of hard-cooked egg, season, and serve.

COOK'S TIP

Mustard has an important place in the salad maker's pantry. Varieties differ from country to country and often suggest particular flavors. This salad has a German slant to it and calls for a sweet and sour German-style mustard. American mustards have a similar quality.

Veal Escalopes with Artichokes

Artichokes are very hard to prepare fresh, so use canned artichoke hearts, instead – they have an excellent flavor and are simple to use.

Serves 4

INGREDIENTS
1 lb veal escalopes
1 shallot
4 oz lean smoked bacon, finely chopped
1 × 14 oz can of artichoke hearts in brine, drained and quartered
⅔ cup veal stock
3 fresh rosemary sprigs
4 tbsp heavy cream
salt and freshly ground black pepper
fresh rosemary sprigs, to garnish

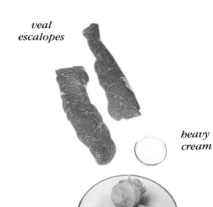

veal escalopes

heavy cream

artichoke hearts

1 Cut the veal into thin slices.

2 Using a sharp knife, cut the shallot into thin slices.

3 Heat the wok, then add the bacon. Stir-fry for 2 minutes. When the fat is released, add the veal and shallot and stir-fry for 3–4 minutes.

4 Add the artichokes and stir-fry for 1 minute. Stir in the stock and rosemary and simmer for 2 minutes. Stir in the heavy cream, season with salt and pepper and serve immediately, garnished with sprigs of fresh rosemary.

Stir-fried Duck with Blueberries

Serve this conveniently quick dinner party dish with sprigs of fresh mint, which will give a wonderful fresh aroma as you bring the meal to the table.

Serves 4

INGREDIENTS
2 duck breasts, about 6 oz each
2 tbsp sunflower oil
1 tbsp red wine vinegar
1 tsp sugar
1 tsp red wine
1 tsp *crème de cassis* (black currant liqueur)
4 oz fresh blueberries
1 tbsp fresh mint, chopped
salt and freshly ground black pepper
fresh mint sprigs, to garnish
mixed green vegetables, steamed, to serve

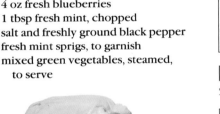

duck

red wine vinegar

blueberries

red wine

mint

1 Cut the duck breasts into neat slices. Season well with salt and pepper.

2 Heat the wok, then add the oil. When the oil is hot, stir-fry the duck for 3 minutes.

3 Add the red wine vinegar, sugar, red wine and *crème de cassis*. Bubble for 3 minutes, to reduce to a thick syrup.

4 Stir in the blueberries, sprinkle over the mint and serve garnished with sprigs of fresh mint.

Pan-fried Pork with Peaches and Green Peppercorns

When peaches are in season, consider this speedy pork dish, brought alive with green peppercorns.

Serves 4

INGREDIENTS
2 cups long-grain rice
4 cups chicken stock
4 × 7 oz pork chops or
    loin pieces
2 tbsp vegetable oil
2 tbsp dark rum or sherry
1 small onion, chopped
3 large ripe peaches
1 tbsp green peppercorns
1 tbsp white wine vinegar
salt and freshly ground black pepper

onion

pork chops

dark rum

oil

green peppercorns

white wine vinegar

peaches

VARIATION

If peaches are not ripe when picked, they can be difficult to peel. Only tree ripened fruit is suitable for peeling. If fresh peaches are out of season, a can of sliced peaches may be used instead.

1 Cover the rice with 3¾ cups chicken stock. Stir, bring to a simmer and cook uncovered for 15 minutes. Switch off the heat and cover for 5 minutes. Season the pork with a generous twist of black pepper. Heat a large bare metal frying pan and moisten the pork with 1 tbsp of the oil. Cook the pork for 12 minutes, turning once.

4 Cover the peaches with boiling water to loosen the skins, then peel, slice and discard the pits.

2 Transfer the meat to a warm plate. Pour off the excess fat from the pan and return to the heat. Allow the sediment to sizzle and brown, add the rum or sherry and loosen the sediment with a flat wooden spoon. Pour the pan contents over the meat, cover and keep warm. Wipe the pan clean.

5 Add the peaches and peppercorns to the onion and coat for 3–4 minutes, until they begin to soften.

3 Heat the remaining vegetable oil in the pan and soften the onion over a steady heat.

6 Add the remaining chicken stock and simmer briefly. Return the pork and meat juices to the pan, sharpen with vinegar, and season to taste. Serve with the rice.

Chicken Roll

The roll can be prepared and cooked the day before and will freeze well too. Remove from the refrigerator about an hour before serving.

Serves 8

INGREDIENTS
1 × 4 lb chicken

FOR THE STUFFING
1 medium onion, finely chopped
4 tbsp melted butter
12 oz lean ground pork
4 rashers lean bacon, chopped
1 tbsp chopped fresh parsley
2 tsp chopped fresh thyme
2 cups fresh white bread crumbs
2 tbsp sherry
1 large egg, beaten
¼ cup shelled unsalted pistachio nuts
¼ cup pitted black olives (about 12)
salt and freshly ground black pepper

1 To make the stuffing, cook the chopped onion gently in 2 tbsp of the butter until soft. Turn into a bowl and cool. Add the remaining ingredients, mix thoroughly and season with salt and freshly ground black pepper.

2 To bone the chicken, use a small, sharp knife to remove the wing tips (pinions). Turn the chicken onto its breast and cut a line down the back bone.

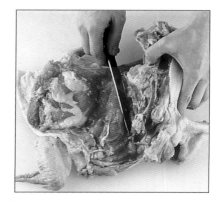

3 Cut the flesh away from the carcass, scraping the bones clean. Carefully cut through the sinew around the leg and wing joints and scrape down the bones to free them. Remove the carcass, taking care not to cut through the skin along the breast bone.

black olives

bread crumbs

thyme

onion

pork

butter

bacon

4 To stuff the chicken, lay it flat, skin side down and level the flesh as much as possible. Shape the stuffing down the center of the chicken and fold the sides over the stuffing.

5 Sew the flesh neatly together, using a needle and dark thread. Tie with fine string into a roll.

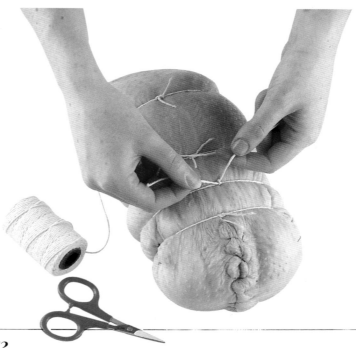

COOK'S TIPS

Thaw the chicken roll from frozen for 12 hours in the refrigerator, and leave to stand at cool room temperature for an hour before serving.

Use dark thread for sewing, as it is much easier to see so that you can remove it once the roll is cooked.

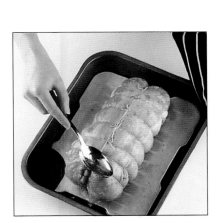

6 Preheat the oven to 350°F. Place the roll, with the join underneath, on a roasting rack in a roasting pan and brush generously with the remaining butter. Bake uncovered for about 1¼ hours or until cooked. Baste the chicken often with the juices in the roasting pan. Leave to cool completely before removing the string and thread. Wrap in foil and chill until ready for serving or freezing.

Swiss Cheese, Chicken, and Tongue Salad with Apple and Celery

The rich sweet flavors of this salad marry well with the tart peppery nature of watercress. A minted lemon dressing combines to freshen the overall effect. Serve with warm new potatoes.

Serves 4

INGREDIENTS

2 free-range chicken breasts, skin and
   bone removed
½ chicken stock cube
½ lb sliced tongue or ham, ¼ in thick
½ lb Swiss cheese
1 lollo rosso lettuce
1 butterhead, Batavian, or Boston
   lettuce
1 bunch watercress
2 green apples, cored and sliced
3 stalks celery, sliced
4 tbsp sesame seeds, toasted
salt, pepper, and nutmeg

DRESSING

5 tbsp peanut or sunflower oil
1 tsp sesame oil
3 tbsp lemon juice
2 tsp chopped fresh mint
3 drops Tabasco sauce

2 To make the dressing, measure the two oils, lemon juice, mint, and Tabasco sauce into a screw-top jar and shake. Cut the chicken, tongue, and cheese into fine strips. Toss with a little dressing and set aside.

3 Wash and spin the salad leaves, combine with the apple and celery, and dress. Distribute between 4 large plates. Pile the chicken, tongue, and cheese in the center, scatter with toasted sesame seeds, season with salt, pepper and freshly grated nutmeg, and serve.

1 Place the chicken breasts in a shallow saucepan, cover with 10 fl oz water, add the ½ stock cube, and bring to a boil. Put the lid on the pan and simmer for 15 minutes. Drain, reserving the stock for another occasion, then cool the chicken under cold running water.

tongue

celery

lollo rosso lettuce

butterhead lettuce

chicken breasts

Swiss cheese

watercress

Chicken Liver, Bacon, and Tomato Salad

Warm salads are especially welcome during the late summer months when the evenings are growing cooler. Try this rich salad with sweet spinach and bitter leaves of frisée lettuce.

Serves 4

INGREDIENTS

½ lb young spinach, stems removed
1 frisée lettuce
7 tbsp peanut or sunflower oil
6 oz bacon, rind removed and cut into strips
3 slices day-old bread, crusts removed and cut into short fingers
1 lb chicken livers
4 oz cherry tomatoes
salt and pepper

2 To make the croutons, fry the bread in the bacon-flavored oil, tossing until crisp and golden. Drain on paper towels.

3 Heat the remaining 3 tbsp of oil in the skillet, add the chicken livers, and fry briskly for 2–3 minutes. Transfer the livers to the salad leaves, add the bacon, croutons, and tomatoes. Season, toss, and serve.

1 Wash and spin the salad leaves. Place in a salad bowl. Heat 4 tbsp of the oil in a large skillet. Add the bacon and cook for 3–4 minutes or until crisp and brown. Remove the bacon with a slotted spoon and drain on a piece of paper towel.

chicken livers

bacon

spinach

cherry tomatoes

bread

Broiled Chicken Salad with Lavender and Sweet Herbs

Lavender may seem like an odd salad ingredient, but its delightful scent has a natural affinity with sweet garlic, orange, and other wild herbs. A serving of cornmeal polenta makes this salad both filling and delicious.

Serves 4

INGREDIENTS
4 boneless chicken breasts
3¾ cups light chicken stock
1 cup fine polenta or cornmeal
2 oz butter
1 lb young spinach
6 oz lamb's lettuce
8 sprigs fresh lavender
8 small tomatoes, halved
salt and pepper

LAVENDER MARINADE
6 fresh lavender flowers
2 tsp finely grated orange zest
2 cloves garlic, crushed
2 tsp clear honey
salt
2 tbsp olive oil, French or Italian
2 tsp chopped fresh thyme
2 tsp chopped fresh marjoram

lavender   *chicken breasts*

polenta   *orange*

spinach

garlic

thyme

1 To make the marinade, strip the lavender flowers from the stems and combine with the orange zest, garlic, honey, and salt. Add the olive oil and herbs. Score the chicken deeply, spread the mixture over the chicken, and leave to marinate in a cool place for at least 20 minutes.

2 To make the polenta, bring the chicken stock to a boil in a heavy saucepan. Add the cornmeal in a steady stream, stirring all the time until thick: this will take 2–3 minutes. Turn the cooked polenta out on to a 1-in-deep buttered tray and allow to cool.

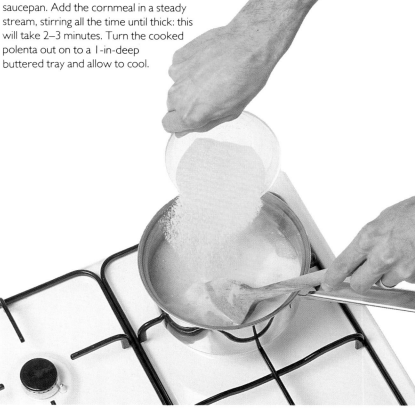

3 Heat the broiler to a moderate temperature. (If using a barbecue, let the embers settle to a steady glow.) Broil the chicken for 15 minutes, turning once.

4 Cut the polenta into 1 in cubes with a wet knife. Heat the butter in a large skillet and fry the polenta until golden.

COOK'S TIP

Lavender marinade is a delicious flavoring for fish as well as chicken. Try it over broiled cod, haddock, halibut, sea bass, and bream.

5 Wash the salad leaves and spin dry, then divide between 4 large plates. Slice each chicken breast and lay over the salad. Place the polenta among the salad, decorate with sprigs of lavender and tomatoes, season and serve.

Tagine of Chicken

Based on a traditional Moroccan dish. The chicken and couscous can be cooked the day before and reheated for serving.

Serves 8

INGREDIENTS
8 chicken legs (thighs and
    drumsticks)
2 tbsp olive oil
1 medium onion, finely chopped
2 garlic cloves, crushed
1 tsp ground turmeric
½ tsp ground ginger
½ tsp ground cinnamon
scant 2 cups fresh or canned chicken
    stock
1¼ cups pitted green olives
1 lemon, sliced
salt and freshly ground black pepper
fresh coriander sprigs, to garnish

FOR THE VEGETABLE COUSCOUS
2½ cups fresh or canned chicken
    stock
1 lb couscous
4 zucchini, thickly sliced
2 carrots, thickly sliced
2 small turnips, peeled and cubed
3 tbsp olive oil
1 × 15 oz can chick peas, drained

onion *green olives* *ginger* *cinnamon* *turmeric* *turnip* *couscous* *lemon* *carrot* *garlic* *coriander* *chick peas* *zucchini* *chicken stock* *olive oil* *chicken*

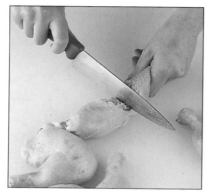

1 Preheat the oven to 350°F. Cut the chicken legs into two through the joint.

2 Heat the oil in a large flameproof casserole and working in batches, brown the chicken on both sides. Remove and keep warm.

3 Add the onion and crushed garlic to the flameproof casserole and cook gently until tender. Add the spices and cook for 1 minute. Pour over the stock, bring to a boil, and return the chicken. Cover and bake for 45 minutes until tender.

4 Transfer the chicken to a bowl, cover and keep warm. Remove any fat from the cooking liquid and boil to reduce by one-third. Meanwhile, blanch the olives and lemon slices in a pan of boiling water for 2 minutes until the lemon skin is tender. Drain and add to the cooking liquid, adjusting the seasoning to taste.

5 To cook the couscous, bring the stock to a boil in a large pan and sprinkle in the couscous slowly, stirring all the time. Remove from the heat, cover and leave to stand for 5 minutes.

COOK'S TIP
The couscous can be reheated with 2 tbsp olive oil in a steamer over a pan of boiling water, stirring occasionally. If you cook the chicken in advance, undercook it by 15 minutes and reheat in the oven for 20–30 minutes.

6 Meanwhile, cook the vegetables, drain and put them into a large bowl. Add the couscous and oil and season. Stir the grains to fluff them up, add the chick peas and finally the chopped coriander. Spoon onto a large serving plate, cover with the chicken pieces, and spoon over the liquid. Garnish with fresh coriander sprigs.

Chicken Liver Kebabs

These may be barbecued outdoors and served with salad and baked potatoes, or broiled indoors and served with rice and broccoli.

Serves 4

INGREDIENTS
4 oz (roughly 6) lean bacon rashers
12 oz trimmed chicken livers
12 large, ready-to-eat pitted prunes
12 cherry tomatoes
8 button mushrooms
2 tbsp olive oil

prunes

olive oil

tomatoes

mushrooms

bacon

chicken livers

1 Cut each rasher of bacon into two pieces, wrap a piece around each chicken liver and secure in position with wooden toothpicks.

2 Wrap the pitted prunes around the cherry tomatoes.

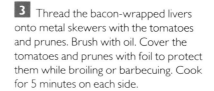

3 Thread the bacon-wrapped livers onto metal skewers with the tomatoes and prunes. Brush with oil. Cover the tomatoes and prunes with foil to protect them while broiling or barbecuing. Cook for 5 minutes on each side.

4 Remove the toothpicks and serve the kebabs immediately.

Citrus Kebabs

Serve on a bed of lettuce leaves and garnish with fresh mint and orange and lemon slices.

Serves 4

INGREDIENTS
4 chicken breasts, skinned and boned
fresh mint sprigs, to garnish
orange, lemon or lime slices, to
garnish (optional)

FOR THE MARINADE
finely grated rind and juice of
½ orange
finely grated rind and juice of ½ small
lemon or lime
2 tbsp olive oil
2 tbsp honey
2 tbsp chopped fresh mint
¼ tsp ground cumin
salt and freshly ground black pepper

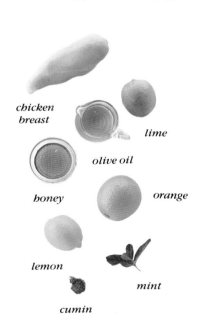

chicken
breast

lime

olive oil

honey

orange

lemon

mint

cumin

1 Cut the chicken into cubes of approximately 1 in.

2 Mix the marinade ingredients together, add the chicken cubes and leave to marinade for at least 2 hours.

3 Thread the chicken pieces onto skewers and broil or barbecue over low coals for 15 minutes, basting with the marinade and turning frequently. Serve garnished with extra mint and citrus slices if desired.

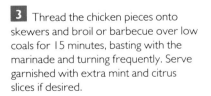

Kotopita

This is based on a Greek chicken pie. Serve hot or cold with a typical Greek salad made from tomatoes, cucumber, onions and feta cheese.

Serves 4

INGREDIENTS
10 oz filo pastry
2 tbsp olive oil
½ cup chopped toasted almonds
2 tbsp milk

FOR THE FILLING
1 tbsp olive oil
1 medium onion, finely chopped
1 garlic clove, crushed
1 lb boned, cooked chicken
2 oz feta cheese, crumbled
2 eggs, beaten
1 tbsp chopped fresh parsley
1 tbsp chopped fresh coriander
1 tbsp chopped fresh mint
salt and freshly ground black pepper

chicken

olive oil

feta cheese

eggs

parsley

almonds

mint

onion

coriander

filo pastry

1 For the filling, heat the oil in a large frying pan and cook the onion gently until tender. Add the garlic clove and cook for a further 2 minutes. Transfer to a bowl.

2 Remove the skin from the chicken and then grind or chop it finely. Add to the onion with the rest of the filling ingredients. Mix thoroughly and season with salt and freshly ground black pepper.

3 Preheat the oven to 375°F. Have a damp dish towel ready to keep the filo pastry covered at all times. You will need to work fast, as the pastry dries out very quickly when exposed to air. Unravel the pastry and cut the whole batch into a 12 in square.

4 Taking half the sheets (cover the remainder), brush one sheet with a little olive oil, lay it on a well greased 2¼ pint ovenproof dish and sprinkle with a few chopped toasted almonds. Repeat with the other sheets, overlapping them alternately into the dish.

5 Spoon in the filling and cover the pie in the same way with the rest of the overlapping pastry.

6 Fold in the overlapping edges and mark a diamond pattern on the surface of the pie with a sharp knife. Brush with milk and sprinkle on any remaining almonds. Bake for 20–30 minutes or until golden brown on top.

Warm Duck Salad with Orange and Cilantro

The rich gamey flavor of duck provides the foundation for this delicious salad. Serve it on summer evenings and enjoy the warm flavor of orange and cilantro.

Serves 4

INGREDIENTS
1 small orange
2 boneless duck breasts
salt and cayenne pepper
²/₃ cup dry white wine
1 tsp ground coriander seeds
½ tsp ground cumin or fennel seeds
2 tbsp superfine sugar
juice of ½ small lime or lemon
3 oz day-old bread, thickly sliced
3 tbsp garlic oil
½ escarole lettuce
½ frisée lettuce
2 tbsp sunflower or peanut oil
4 sprigs fresh cilantro

1 Halve the orange and slice thickly. Discard any stray seeds and place the slices in a small saucepan. Cover with water, bring to a boil, and simmer for 5 minutes to remove the bitterness. Drain and set aside.

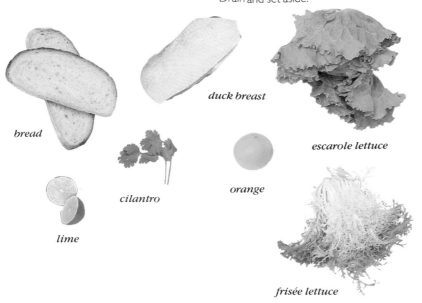

bread

duck breast

cilantro

orange

escarole lettuce

lime

frisée lettuce

2 Pierce the skin of the duck breasts diagonally with a small knife (this will help release the fat as they cook). Rub the skin with salt. Place a steel or cast-iron skillet over a steady heat and cook the breasts for 20 minutes, turning once, until they are medium-rare. Transfer to a warm plate, cover, and keep warm. Pour the duck fat into a small bowl and set aside for use on another occasion.

3 Heat the sediment in the skillet until it begins to darken and caramelize. Add the wine and stir to loosen the sediment. Add the ground coriander, cumin, sugar, and orange slices. Boil quickly and reduce to a coating consistency. Sharpen with lime juice and season to taste with salt and cayenne pepper. Transfer to a bowl, cover, and keep warm.

4 To make the garlic croutons, remove the crusts from the bread and discard them. Cut the bread into short fingers. Heat the garlic oil in a heavy skillet and brown until evenly crisp. Season with salt, then drain on paper towels.

5 Wash the salad leaves and spin dry. Toss with sunflower oil and distribute between 4 large serving plates.

6 Slice the duck breasts diagonally with a carving knife. Divide the breast meat into 4 and lift on to each salad plate. Spoon on the dressing, scatter with croutons, decorate with a sprig of cilantro and serve.

COOK'S TIP
Duck breast has the quality of red meat and is cooked either rare, medium, or well-done according to taste.

Minty Lamb Burgers with Red-currant Chutney

These rather special burgers take a little extra time to prepare, but are well worth it.

COOK'S TIP
If time is short, or if fresh red currants are not available, serve the burgers with red-currant sauce from a jar.

Serves 4

1¼ lb lean ground lamb
1 small onion, finely chopped
2 tbsp finely chopped fresh mint
2 tbsp finely chopped fresh parsley
4 oz mozzarella cheese
salt and freshly ground black pepper

FOR THE CHUTNEY
1½ cups fresh or frozen red currants
2 tsp honey
1 tsp balsamic vinegar
2 tbsp finely chopped mint

red currants

mint

balsamic vinegar

ground lamb

honey

mozzarella cheese

parsley

onion

1 Mix together the lamb, onion, mint and parsley until evenly combined; season well with salt and pepper.

2 Divide the mixture into eight equal pieces and use your hands to press them into flat rounds.

3 Cut the mozzarella into four slices or cubes. Place them on four of the lamb rounds. Top each with another round of meat mixture.

4 Press together firmly, making four flat burger shapes and sealing in the cheese completely.

5 Place all the ingredients for the chutney in a bowl and mash them together with a fork. Season well with salt and pepper.

6 Brush the lamb patties with oil and cook them over a moderately hot barbecue for about 15 minutes, turning once, until golden brown. Serve with the red-currant chutney.

Grilled Mediterranean Vegetables with Marbled Yogurt Pesto

Char-grilled summer vegetables served with a pesto sauce – a meal on its own, or served with grilled meats and fish.

Serves 4

2 small eggplants
2 large zucchini
1 red bell pepper
1 yellow bell pepper
1 fennel bulb
1 red onion
olive oil for brushing

FOR THE SAUCE
²/₃ cup plain yogurt
3 tbsp pesto
salt and freshly ground black
    pepper

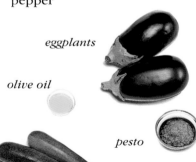

eggplants

olive oil

pesto

zucchini

yogurt

fennel

red pepper

red onion   *yellow pepper*

COOK'S TIP

Baby vegetables make excellent candidates for grilling whole, so look out for baby eggplants and peppers, in particular. There's no need to salt the eggplants, if they're small.

1 Cut the eggplants into ¹/₂ in thick slices. Sprinkle with salt and allow to drain for about 30 minutes. Rinse and dry well.

2 Cut the zucchini in half lengthwise. Cut the peppers in half, remove the seeds but leave the stalk on.

3 Slice the fennel and the onion into thick wedges.

4 Stir the yogurt and pesto lightly together, to make a marbled sauce. Spoon into a serving bowl.

5 Arrange the vegetables on the hot barbecue, brush with oil and sprinkle with salt and pepper.

6 Cook the vegetables until golden brown and tender, turning occasionally. The eggplants and peppers will take 6–8 minutes to cook, the zucchini, onion and fennel 4–5 minutes. Serve with the marbled pesto sauce.

Peppered Steaks in Beer and Garlic

Robust flavors for hearty appetites. Serve with salad and baked potatoes.

Serves 4

4 beef sirloin or rump steaks,
  1 in thick, about 6 oz each
2 garlic cloves, crushed
½ cup brown ale or stout
2 tbsp dark raw sugar
2 tbsp Worcestershire sauce
1 tbsp corn oil
1 tbsp crushed black
  peppercorns

dark raw sugar

brown ale

steaks

Worcestershire sauce

garlic

corn oil

black peppercorns

COOK'S TIP

Take care when basting with the reserved marinade, as the alcohol will tend to flare up; spoon or brush on just a small amount at a time.

1 Place the steaks in a deep dish and add the garlic, ale or stout, sugar, Worcestershire sauce and oil. Turn to coat evenly in the marinade, and then allow to marinate in the refrigerator for 2–3 hours or overnight.

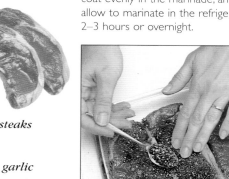

2 Remove the steaks from the dish and reserve the marinade. Sprinkle the peppercorns over the steaks and press them into the surface.

3 Cook the steaks on a hot barbecue, basting them occasionally during cooking, with the reserved marinade.

4 Turn the steaks once during cooking, and cook them for 3–6 minutes on each side, depending on how rare you like them.

Indonesian Pork and Peanut Saté

These delicious skewers of pork are popular street food in Indonesia. They are quick to make and eat.

Serves 4

INGREDIENTS
2 cups long-grain rice
1 lb lean pork
pinch of salt
2 limes, quartered, to garnish
4 oz green salad, to serve

FOR THE BASTE AND DIP
1 tbsp vegetable oil
1 small onion, chopped
1 garlic clove, crushed
½ tsp hot chili sauce
1 tbsp sugar
2 tbsp soy sauce
2 tbsp lemon or lime juice
½ tsp anchovy paste (optional)
4 tbsp smooth peanut butter

lemon

lime

rice

peanut butter

pork

garlic

chili sauce

1 In a large saucepan, cover the rice with 3¾ cups of boiling salted water, stir and simmer uncovered for 15 minutes until the liquid has been absorbed. Switch off the heat, cover and stand for 5 minutes. Slice the pork into thin strips, then thread zig-zag fashion onto 16 bamboo skewers.

2 Heat the vegetable oil in a pan. Add the onion and cook over a gentle heat to soften without coloring for about 3–4 minutes. Add the next 5 ingredients and the anchovy paste, if using. Simmer briefly, then stir in the peanut butter.

3 Preheat a moderate broiler, spoon a third of the sauce over the pork and cook for 6–8 minutes, turning once. Spread the rice out onto a serving dish, place the pork saté on top and serve with the dipping sauce. Garnish with quartered limes and serve with a green salad.

VARIATION
Indonesian saté can be prepared with lean beef, chicken or shrimp.

Broiled Chicken with Pica de Gallo Salsa

This dish originates from Mexico. Its hot fruity flavors form the essence of Tex-Mex Cooking.

COOK'S TIP
To capture the spirit of Tex-Mex food, cook the chicken over a barbecue and eat shaded from the hot summer sun.

Serves 4

INGREDIENTS
4 chicken breasts
pinch of celery salt and cayenne
    pepper combined
2 tbsp vegetable oil
corn chips, to serve

FOR THE SALSA
10 oz watermelon
6 oz canteloupe melon
1 small red onion
1–2 green chilies
2 tbsp lime juice
4 tbsp chopped fresh cilantro
pinch of salt

green chilies

chicken breasts

red onion

lime

cilantro

canteloupe melon

watermelon

1 Preheat a moderate broiler. Slash the chicken breasts deeply to speed up the cooking time.

2 Season the chicken with celery salt and cayenne, brush with oil and broil for about 15 minutes.

3 To make the salsa, remove the rind and as many seeds as you can from the melons. Finely dice the flesh and put it into a bowl.

4 Finely chop the onion, split the chilies (discarding the seeds which contain most of the heat) and chop. Take care not to touch sensitive skin areas when handling cut chilies. Mix with the melon.

5 Add the lime juice and chopped cilantro, and season with a pinch of salt. Turn the salsa into a small bowl.

6 Arrange the grilled chicken on a plate and serve with the salsa and a handful of corn chips.

Mexican Beef Burgers

Nothing beats the flavor and quality of a home-made burger. This version is from Mexico and is seasoned with cumin and fresh cilantro.

Makes 4

INGREDIENTS
4 ears of corn
1 cup stale white bread crumbs
6 tbsp milk
1 small onion, finely chopped
1 tsp ground cumin
½ tsp cayenne pepper
½ tsp celery salt
3 tbsp chopped fresh cilantro
2 lb lean ground beef
4 sesame buns
4 tbsp mayonnaise
4 tomato slices
½ iceberg lettuce or other leaves
    such as frisée or Romaine
salt and freshly ground black pepper
1 large packet corn chips,
    to serve

iceberg lettuce

ground beef

onion

tomatoes

sesame buns

white bread

1 Bring a large saucepan of water to a boil, add a good pinch of salt and cook the corn for 15 minutes.

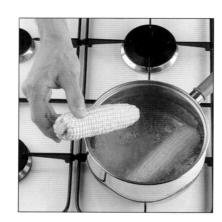

2 Combine the bread crumbs, milk, onion, cumin, cayenne, celery salt and fresh cilantro in a large bowl.

3 Add the beef and mix by hand until evenly blended.

4 Divide the beef mixture into four portions and flatten between sheets of plastic wrap.

5 Preheat a moderate broiler and cook for 10 minutes for medium burgers or 15 minutes for well-done burgers, turning once during the cooking time.

6 Split and toast the buns, spread with mayonnaise and sandwich the burgers with the tomato slices, lettuce leaves and seasoning. Serve with corn chips and the ears of corn.

COOK'S TIP
If planning ahead, freeze the burgers between sheets of wax paper or plastic wrap. Covered, they will keep well for up to twelve weeks. Defrost before cooking.

Minted Egg and Fennel Tabbouleh with Toasted Hazelnuts

Tabbouleh, a Middle Eastern dish of steamed bulghur wheat, is suited to warm-weather picnics.

Serves 4

INGREDIENTS
1¼ cups bulghur wheat
2 eggs
1 bulb fennel
1 bunch scallions, chopped
1 oz sun-dried tomatoes, sliced
3 tbsp chopped fresh parsley
2 tbsp chopped fresh mint
3 oz black olives
4 tbsp olive oil, preferably Greek or
    Spanish
2 tbsp garlic oil
2 tbsp lemon juice
salt and pepper
1 romaine lettuce
about 1 cup chopped hazelnuts,
    toasted
1 medium open-textured loaf or 4 pita
    breads, warmed

2 Boil the eggs for 12 minutes. Cool under running water, shell, and quarter. Halve and finely slice the fennel. Boil in salted water for 6 minutes, drain, and cool under running water. Combine the eggs, fennel, scallions, sun-dried tomatoes, parsley, mint, and olives with the bulghur wheat. Dress with olive oil, garlic oil, and lemon juice. Season well.

3 Wash the lettuce leaves and spin dry. Line an attractive salad bowl or plate with the leaves, pile in the tabbouleh, and scatter with toasted hazelnuts. Serve with a basket of warm bread.

1 Cover the bulghur wheat with boiling water and leave to soak for 15 minutes. Transfer to a metal strainer, position over a saucepan of boiling water, cover, and steam for 10 minutes. Spread out on a metal tray and leave to cool.

COOK'S TIP

A popular way to eat tabbouleh is to shovel it into pockets of pita bread.

romaine lettuce

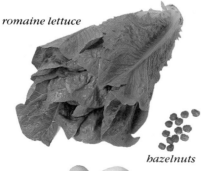

hazelnuts

eggs

mint

olives

parsley

fennel

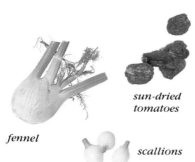

sun-dried tomatoes

scallions

Chinese Chicken Wings

These are best eaten with fingers as a first course, so make sure you provide finger bowls and plenty of paper napkins.

Serves 4

INGREDIENTS
12 chicken wings
3 garlic cloves, crushed
2 tsp grated fresh ginger root
juice of 1 large lemon
3 tbsp soy sauce
3 tbsp honey
½ tsp chili powder
⅔ cup fresh or canned chicken stock
salt and fresh ground black pepper
lemon wedges, to garnish

garlic

lemon

chicken wings

soy sauce

honey *chili powder*

ginger

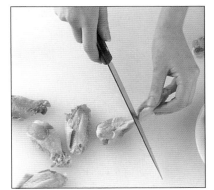

1 Remove the wing tips (pinions) and use to make the stock. Cut the wings into two joints.

2 Mix the remaining ingredients together and coat the chicken pieces in the mixture completely. Cover with plastic wrap and marinate overnight.

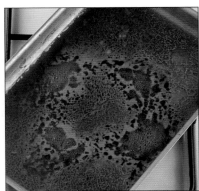

3 Preheat the oven to 425°F. Remove the wings from the marinade and arrange in a single layer in a roasting pan. Bake for 20–25 minutes, basting at least twice with the marinade during cooking until all the marinade is used up.

4 Place the wings on a serving plate. Add the stock to the marinade in the roasting pan, and bring to a boil. Cook to a syrupy consistency and spoon a little over the wings. Serve garnished with lemon wedges.

Koftas

A fun way to serve spicy ground lamb. These tasty kebabs are packed with flavors from the Mediterranean.

Serves 4

INGREDIENTS
1 lb/4 cups ground lamb
1½ cups fresh whole wheat bread
    crumbs
1 onion, grated
1 tsp ground cumin
2 garlic cloves, crushed
1 egg, beaten
¼ cup lamb stock
salt and freshly ground black pepper

bread crumbs

egg

garlic

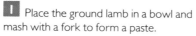

cumin

ground lamb

onion

1 Place the ground lamb in a bowl and mash with a fork to form a paste.

2 Add the bread crumbs and onion.

3 Stir in the cumin and garlic. Season well to taste.

4 Stir in the egg and stock with a fork. Using your hands bind the mixture together until smooth.

5 Shape into "sausages" with lightly floured hands.

COOK'S TIP
Soak the wooden skewers in cold water for 30 minutes before using to prevent them from burning.

6 Thread onto wooden kebab skewers and broil under a medium heat for 30 minutes, turning occasionally. Serve with a crisp green salad.

Chicken and Stilton Pies

A tasty filling of chicken and Stilton is wrapped in a crisp pastry crust to make four individual pies. They can be served hot or cold.

Makes 4

INGREDIENTS
3 cups self-rising flour
½ tsp salt
6 tbsp lard
6 tbsp butter
5 tbsp cold water
beaten egg, to glaze

FOR THE FILLING
1 lb boned and skinned chicken thighs
¼ cup chopped walnuts
1 oz scallions, sliced
½ cup Stilton, crumbled
1 oz celery, finely chopped
½ tsp dried thyme
salt and freshly ground black pepper

scallions

butter

celery

Stilton

thyme

flour

chicken thighs

1 Preheat the oven to 400°F. Mix the flour and salt in a bowl. Rub in the lard and butter with your fingers until the mixture resembles fine bread crumbs. Using a knife to cut and stir, mix in the cold water to form a stiff, pliable dough. Chill for 1 hour if possible.

2 Turn out onto a worktop and knead lightly until smooth. Divide into four equal pieces and roll out each piece to a thickness of ¼ in, keeping a good round shape. Cut into an 8 in circle, using a plate as a guide.

3 Remove any fat from the chicken thighs and cut into small cubes. Mix with the walnuts, scallions, Stilton, celery, thyme and seasoning and divide between the four pastry circles.

4 Brush the edge of the pastry with beaten egg and fold over, pinching and crimping the edges together well. Place on a greased baking sheet and bake in the preheated oven for about 45 minutes or until golden brown.

Tandoori Chicken

A popular party dish. The chicken is marinated the night before so all you have to do on the day is to cook it in a very hot oven and serve with wedges of lemon and green salad.

Serves 4

INGREDIENTS

1 × 3½ lb chicken, cut into 8 pieces
juice of 1 large lemon
⅔ cup plain low fat yogurt
3 garlic cloves, crushed
2 tbsp olive oil
1 tsp ground turmeric
2 tsp ground paprika
1 tsp grated fresh ginger root or
⠀⠀½ tsp ground ginger
2 tsp garam masala
1 tsp salt
a few drops of red food coloring
⠀⠀(optional)

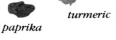

lemon

garlic

olive oil

ginger

yogurt

garam masala

chicken

turmeric

paprika

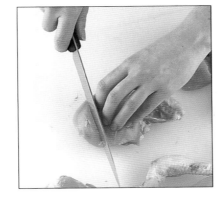

1 Skin the chicken pieces and cut two slits in each piece.

2 Arrange in a single layer in a dish and pour over the lemon juice.

3 Mix together the remaining ingredients and pour the sauce over the chicken pieces, turning them to coat thoroughly. Cover with plastic wrap and chill overnight.

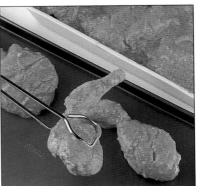

4 Preheat the oven to 425°F. Remove the chicken from the marinade and arrange in a single layer in a shallow baking sheet. Bake for 15 minutes, turn over, and cook for a further 15 minutes or until tender.

Spicy Barbecued Salmon

If you intend to barbecue the salmon, make sure the barbecue is heated up thoroughly before you start to cook. It should take the same cooking time as conventional broiling.

Serves 4

INGREDIENTS
1 small red onion
1 garlic clove
6 plum tomatoes
2 tbsp butter
3 tbsp tomato ketchup
2 tbsp Dijon mustard
2 tbsp dark brown sugar
1 tbsp honey
1 tsp ground cayenne pepper
1 tbsp ancho chili powder
1 tbsp ground paprika
1 tbsp Worcestershire sauce
4 × 6 oz salmon fillets

cayenne pepper

Dijon mustard

dark brown sugar

plum tomato

red onion

salmon fillet

tomato ketchup

1 Finely chop the red onion and finely dice the garlic.

2 Dice the tomatoes.

3 Melt the butter in a large, heavy-based saucepan and gently cook the onion and garlic until translucent.

4 Add the tomatoes and simmer for 15 minutes.

5 Add the remaining ingredients except the salmon and simmer for a further 20 minutes. Process the mixture in a food processor fitted with a metal blade and leave to cool.

6 Brush the salmon with the sauce and chill for at least 2 hours. Barbecue or broil for about 2–3 minutes either side, brushing on the sauce when necessary.

Stilton Burger

Slightly more up-market than the traditional burger, this tasty recipe contains a delicious surprise. The lightly melted Stilton cheese encased in a crunchy burger is absolutely delicious.

Serves 4

INGREDIENTS
1 lb/4 cups ground beef
1 onion, finely chopped
1 celery stalk, chopped
1 tsp dried mixed herbs
1 tsp prepared mustard
½ cup crumbled Stilton cheese
4 burger buns
salt and freshly ground black pepper

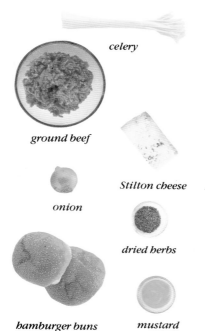

celery

ground beef

Stilton cheese

onion

dried herbs

hamburger buns

mustard

1 Place the ground beef in a bowl together with the onion and celery. Season well.

2 Stir in the herbs and mustard, bringing them together to form a firm mixture.

3 Divide the mixture into eight equal portions. Place four on a chopping board and flatten each one slightly.

4 Place the crumbled cheese in the center of each.

5 Flatten the remaining mixture and place on top. Mold the mixture together encasing the crumbled cheese and shape into four burgers.

6 Grill under a medium heat for 10 minutes, turning once or until cooked through. Split the hamburger buns and place a burger inside each. Serve with salad, ketchup, and mustard pickle.

Salami Hero

This is a huge affair, filled with as much as you can cram into a roll. Fillings vary by region: tuna, egg, cheese, coleslaw, salads, meats, or salami, but there are no hard and fast rules. Fill according to your taste or availability.

Makes 2

INGREDIENTS
2 long crusty rolls
2 tbsp softened butter
few leaves lollo rosso lettuce or
    radicchio
3 oz coleslaw
3 oz Italian salami, sliced
1 tomato, sliced
2 tbsp mayonnaise

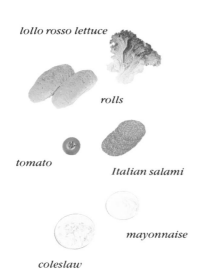

lollo rosso lettuce

rolls

tomato

Italian salami

mayonnaise

coleslaw

1 Cut the rolls horizontally three-quarters of the way through, open out sufficiently to take the filling, and butter both cut sides.

2 Arrange lettuce or radicchio leaves on the base, then add a spoonful of coleslaw.

3 Fold the salami slices in half and arrange over the top. Cover with a little more lettuce, tomato slices, and a little mayonnaise. Serve with a napkin!

Classic BLT

This delicious American favorite is made with crispy fried bacon, lettuce, and tomato. Choose the bread you prefer and toast it if you like.

Makes 2

INGREDIENTS
4 slices multi-grain bread
1 tbsp softened butter
8 slices bacon
few crisp lettuce leaves, romaine or
    iceberg
1 large tomato, sliced
2 tbsp mayonnaise

multi-grain bread

tomato

lettuce

bacon

1 Spread 2 of the slices of bread with butter. Lay the lettuce over the bread and cover with sliced tomato.

2 Broil or fry the bacon until it begins to crisp, then arrange it over the sliced tomato.

3 Spread the 2 remaining slices of bread with mayonnaise. Lay over the bacon, press the sandwich together gently, and cut in half.

Pan Bagna

This literally means 'bathed bread' and is basically a Salade Niçoise stuffed into a baguette or roll. The olive oil dressing soaks into the bread when it is left for an hour or so with a weight on top of it.

Makes 4

INGREDIENTS
1 large baguette
⅔ cup French Dressing
1 small onion, thinly sliced
3 tomatoes, sliced
1 small green or red bell pepper, seeded and sliced
2 oz can anchovy fillets, drained
3½ oz can tuna fish, drained
2 oz black olives, halved and pitted

baguette

French Dressing

bell peppers

tomatoes

tuna fish

onion

anchovy fillets

olives

I Split the baguette horizontally along one side without cutting all the way through the crust.

2 Open the bread out so that it lies flat and sprinkle the French Dressing evenly over the top.

3 Arrange the onion, tomatoes, green or red pepper, anchovies, tuna, and olives on one side of the bread. Close the 2 halves, pressing firmly together.

4 Wrap in plastic wrap, lay a board on top, put a weight on it, and leave for about 1 hour: as well as allowing the dressing to soak into the bread, this makes it easier to eat.

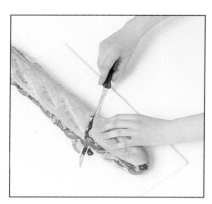

5 Cut the loaf diagonally into 4 equal portions.

FRENCH DRESSING

Olive oil is a must for this dressing; it imparts a rich, fruity flavor, especially if you use that lovely green, virgin olive oil. Make a large quantity at a time and store it in a wine bottle, ready for instant use.

Makes about scant 2 cups

1½ cups extra-virgin olive oil
6 tbsp red-wine vinegar
1 tbsp Moutarde de Meaux
1 garlic clove, crushed
1 tsp clear honey
salt and pepper

Pour the olive oil into a measuring jug and make up to a scant 2 cups with the vinegar. Add the remaining ingredients, then, using a funnel pour into a wine bottle. Put in the cork firmly, give the mixture a thorough shake, and store.

Farmer's Brunch

A new and tasty twist to a traditional British snack. Use very fresh crusty white bread and top the cheese with a homemade Peach Relish, which goes especially well with Red Leicester cheese.

Makes 2

INGREDIENTS
4 slices crusty white bread
2 tbsp softened butter
¼ lb Red Leicester or Wensleydale cheese (or use Monterey Jack or Tilamook), sliced
3 tbsp Peach Relish
scallions or pickled onions, and tomato wedges, to serve

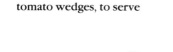

white bread

Red Leicester

tomato

scallion

Peach Relish

1 Butter the bread.

2 Cover 2 slices with cheese.

3 Spread Peach Relish over the remaining 2 slices and place them over the cheese.

4 Cut in half and serve with scallions or pickled onions, and tomato wedges.

PEACH RELISH

A very quick relish that can be eaten immediately. It will keep up to 1 month in the refrigerator.

Makes about 3 cups relish

4 tbsp wine vinegar
4 tbsp light brown sugar
1 tsp finely chopped chili
1 tsp finely chopped ginger
5 peaches, pitted and chopped
1 yellow bell pepper, seeded and chopped
1 small onion, chopped

Put the vinegar and sugar in a saucepan with the chili and ginger and heat gently until the sugar has dissolved.

Add the remaining ingredients and bring to a boil, stirring constantly.

Cover and cook gently for 15 minutes. Remove the lid and cook for 10–15 minutes more, until tender and the liquid is slightly reduced. Pour into clean, warm jars and cover.

Cannelloni

This Italian dish has fast become popular, offering many variations to the original recipe. This version introduces a variety of vegetables which are topped with a traditional cheese sauce.

Serves 4

INGREDIENTS
8 cannelloni tubes
4 oz spinach

FOR THE FILLING
1 tbsp oil
1½ cups ground beef
2 garlic cloves, crushed
2 tbsp flour
½ cup beef stock
1 small carrot, finely chopped
1 small yellow squash, chopped
salt and freshly ground black pepper

FOR THE SAUCE
2 tbsp butter
2 tbsp flour
1 cup milk
½ cup freshly grated Parmesan cheese

spinach

ground beef

cannelloni

garlic

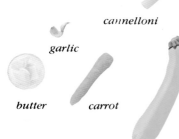
butter   *carrot*

squash

Parmesan cheese

1 Preheat the oven to 350°F. For the filling, heat the oil in a large pan. Add the ground beef and garlic. Cook for 5 minutes.

2 Add the flour and cook for a further 1 minute. Slowly stir in the stock and bring to a boil.

3 Add the carrot and squash, season well and cook for 10 minutes.

4 Spoon the beef mixture into the cannelloni tubes and place in an ovenproof dish.

5 Blanch the spinach in boiling water for 3 minutes. Drain well and place on top of the cannelloni tubes.

6 For the sauce melt the butter in a pan. Add the flour and cook for 1 minute. Pour in the milk, add the grated cheese and season well. Bring to a boil, stirring all the time. Pour over the cannelloni and spinach and cook for 30 minutes in the preheated oven. Serve with tomatoes and a crisp green salad.

Pasta Bows with Smoked Salmon and Dill

In Italy, pasta cooked with smoked salmon is becoming very fashionable. This is a quick and luxurious sauce.

Serves 4

INGREDIENTS
6 scallions, sliced
4 tbsp butter
6 tbsp dry white wine or vermouth
2 cups heavy cream
salt and pepper
freshly grated nutmeg
½ lb smoked salmon
2 tbsp chopped fresh dill or 1 tbsp dried dill
freshly squeezed lemon juice
1 lb pasta bows (farfalle)

pasta bows

lemon

scallions

smoked salmon

nutmeg

dill

1 Slice the scallions finely. Melt the butter in a saucepan and fry the scallions for 1 minute until softened.

2 Add the wine and boil hard to reduce to about 2 tbsp. Stir in the cream and add salt, pepper, and nutmeg to taste. Bring to a boil and simmer for 2–3 minutes until slightly thickened.

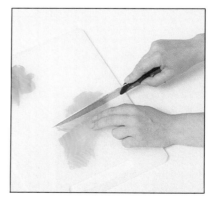

3 Cut the smoked salmon into 1 in squares and stir into the sauce with the dill. Taste and add a little lemon juice. Keep warm.

4 Cook the pasta in plenty of boiling salted water according to the manufacturer's instructions. Drain well. Toss the pasta with the sauce and serve immediately.

Stir-fried Vegetables with Pasta

This is a colorful Chinese-style dish, easily prepared using pasta instead of Chinese noodles.

Serves 4

INGREDIENTS
1 medium carrot
6 oz small zucchini
6 oz green beans
6 oz baby corn
1 lb ribbon pasta such as tagliatelle
salt
2 tbsp corn oil, plus extra for tossing
    the pasta
½ in piece fresh ginger, peeled and
    finely chopped
2 garlic cloves, finely chopped
6 tbsp yellow bean sauce
6 scallions, sliced into 1 in lengths
2 tbsp dry sherry
1 tsp sesame seeds

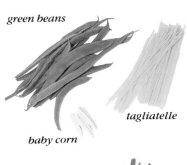

green beans

tagliatelle

baby corn

ginger   *scallions*

zucchini   *garlic*

1 Slice the carrot and zucchini diagonally into chunks. Slice the beans diagonally. Cut the baby corn diagonally in half.

2 Cook the pasta in plenty of boiling salted water according to the manufacturer's instructions, drain, then rinse under hot water. Toss in a little oil.

3 Heat 2 tbsp oil until smóking in a wok or skillet and add the ginger and garlic. Stir-fry for 30 seconds, then add the carrots, beans, and zucchini.

4 Stir-fry for 3–4 minutes, then stir in the yellow bean sauce. Stir-fry for 2 minutes, add the scallions, sherry, and pasta and stir-fry for 1 minute more until piping hot. Sprinkle with sesame seeds and serve immediately.

Penne with Eggplant and Mint Pesto

This splendid variation on the classic Italian pesto uses fresh mint rather than basil for a different flavor.

Serves 4

INGREDIENTS
2 large eggplants
salt
1 lb penne
2 oz walnut halves

FOR THE PESTO
1 oz fresh mint
½ oz flat-leaf parsley
1½ oz walnuts
1½ oz Parmesan cheese, finely grated
2 garlic cloves
6 tbsp olive oil
salt and freshly ground black pepper

penne

garlic

walnuts

eggplant

olive oil

parsley

mint

Parmesan

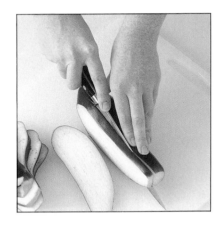

1 Cut the eggplants lengthwise into 1 cm/½ in slices.

2 Cut the slices again crosswise to give short strips.

3 Layer the strips in a colander with salt and leave to stand for 30 minutes over a plate to catch any juices. Rinse well in cool water and drain.

4 Place all the pesto ingredients except the oil in a blender or food processor, blend until smooth, then gradually add the oil in a thin stream until the mixture comes together. Season to taste.

5 Cook the penne following the instructions on the side of the package for about 8 minutes or until nearly cooked. Add the eggplant and cook for a further 3 minutes.

6 Drain well and mix in the mint pesto and walnut halves. Serve immediately.

Margherita Pizza

(Tomato, Basil and Mozzarella)
This classic pizza is simple to prepare. The sweet flavour of sun-ripened tomatoes works wonderfully with the basil and mozzarella.

Serves 2–3

INGREDIENTS
1 pizza base, about 10–12 in
   diameter
2 tbsp olive oil
1 quantity Tomato Sauce
5 oz mozzarella
2 ripe tomatoes, thinly sliced
6–8 fresh basil leaves
2 tbsp freshly grated Parmesan
black pepper

basil

mozzarella

Parmesan

olive oil

Tomato Sauce

tomatoes

1 Preheat the oven to 425°F. Brush the pizza base with 1 tbsp of the oil and then spread over the Tomato Sauce.

2 Cut the mozzarella into thin slices.

3 Arrange the sliced mozzarella and tomatoes on top of the pizza base.

4 Roughly tear the basil leaves, add and sprinkle with the Parmesan. Drizzle over the remaining oil and season with black pepper. Bake for 15–20 minutes until crisp and golden. Serve immediately.

Marinara Pizza

(Tomato and Garlic)
The combination of garlic, good quality olive oil and oregano give this pizza an unmistakably Italian flavor.

Serves 2–3

INGREDIENTS
4 tbsp olive oil
1½ lb plum tomatoes, peeled, seeded
   and chopped
1 pizza base, about 10–12 in
   diameter
4 garlic cloves, cut into slivers
1 tbsp chopped fresh oregano
salt and black pepper

olive oil

oregano

plum tomatoes

garlic

1 Preheat the oven to 425°F. Heat 2 tbsp of the oil in a pan. Add the tomatoes and cook, stirring frequently for about 5 minutes until soft.

2 Place the tomatoes in a strainer and leave to drain for about 5 minutes.

3 Transfer the tomatoes to a food processor or blender and purée until smooth.

4 Brush the pizza base with half the remaining oil. Spoon over the tomatoes and sprinkle with garlic and oregano. Drizzle over the remaining oil and season. Bake for 15–20 minutes until crisp and golden. Serve immediately.

American Hot Pizza

This popular pizza is spiced with green chilies and pepperoni.

Serves 2–3

INGREDIENTS

1 pizza base, about 10–12 in
   diameter
1 tbsp olive oil
4 oz can peeled and chopped green
   chilies in brine, drained
1 quantity Tomato Sauce
3 oz sliced pepperoni
6 pitted black olives
1 tbsp chopped fresh oregano
4 oz mozzarella, grated
oregano leaves, to garnish

mozzarella

oregano

Tomato Sauce

pepperoni

olive oil

green chillies

black olives

1 Preheat the oven to 425°F. Brush the pizza base with the oil.

2 Stir the chilies into the sauce, and spread over the base.

3 Sprinkle the pepperoni over.

4 Halve the olives lengthwise and sprinkle over, with the oregano.

5 Sprinkle the grated mozzarella over and bake for 15–20 minutes until the pizza is crisp and golden.

COOK'S TIP

To make enough Tomato Sauce to cover a 10–12 in round pizza base: Heat 1 tbsp olive oil in a pan, add 1 finely chopped onion, and 1 crushed garlic clove. Gently fry for about 5 minutes then add a 14 oz can chopped tomatoes, 1 tbsp tomato paste, 1 tbsp chopped fresh mixed herbs, and a pinch each of sugar, salt and black pepper. Simmer for about 20 minutes or until the sauce is thick. Let cool completely before use.

6 Garnish with oregano leaves and serve immediately.

Capellini with Arugula, Snow Peas and Pine Nuts

A light but filling pasta dish with the added pepperiness of fresh arugula.

Serves 4

INGREDIENTS
9 oz capellini or angel-hair pasta
8 oz snow peas
6 oz arugula
¼ cup pine nuts, roasted
2 tbsp Parmesan cheese, finely grated (optional)
2 tbsp olive oil (optional)

arugula

Parmesan

pine nuts

capellini

snow peas

1 Cook the capellini or angel-hair pasta following the instructions on the side of the package until *al dente*.

2 Meanwhile, carefully top and tail the snow peas.

3 As soon as the pasta is cooked, drop in the arugula and snow peas. Drain immediately.

4 Toss the pasta with the roasted pine nuts, and Parmesan and olive oil if using. Serve at once.

COOK'S TIP
Olive oil and Parmesan are optional as they obviously raise the fat content.

Pasta Bows with Fennel and Walnut Sauce

A scrumptious blend of walnuts and crisp steamed fennel.

Serves 4

INGREDIENTS

½ cup walnuts, shelled and roughly chopped
1 garlic clove
1 oz fresh flat-leaf parsley leaves, picked from the stems
½ cup ricotta cheese
1 lb pasta bows
1 lb fennel bulbs
chopped walnuts, to garnish

garlic

pasta bows

ricotta

fennel

parsley

walnut halves

chopped walnuts

1 Place the chopped walnuts, garlic and parsley in a food processor. Pulse until roughly chopped. Transfer to a bowl and stir in the ricotta.

2 Cook the pasta following the instructions on the side of the package until *al dente*. Drain well.

3 Slice the fennel thinly and steam for 4–5 minutes until just tender but still crisp.

4 Return the pasta to the pan and add the walnut mixture and the fennel. Toss well and sprinkle with the chopped walnuts. Serve immediately.

Sun-dried Tomato Bread

This savory bread tastes delicious on its own, but it also makes exceptional sandwiches.

Makes 1 loaf

INGREDIENTS
3¼ cups bread flour
1 tsp salt
2 tsp rapid-rise dried yeast
2 oz (drained weight) sun-dried
    tomatoes in oil, chopped
¾ cup lukewarm water
5 tbsp lukewarm olive oil, plus extra
    for brushing
plain flour for dusting

water

flour

olive oil

rapid-rise yeast

sun-dried tomatoes

salt

1 Sift the flour and salt into a large mixing bowl.

2 Stir in the yeast and sun-dried tomatoes.

3 Make a well in the center of the dry ingredients. Pour in the water and oil, and mix until the ingredients come together and form a soft dough.

4 Turn the dough on to a lightly floured surface and knead for about 10 minutes.

5 Shape into an oblong loaf, without making the top too smooth, and place on a greased baking sheet. Brush the top with oil, cover with plastic wrap, then let rise in a warm place for about 1 hour.

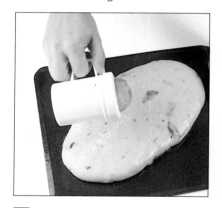

6 Meanwhile, preheat the oven to 425°F. Remove the plastic wrap, then sprinkle the top of the loaf lightly with flour. Bake for 30–40 minutes until the loaf sounds hollow when tapped on the bottom. Serve warm.

Rosemary and Sea Salt Focaccia

Focaccia is an Italian flat bread made with olive oil. Here it is given added flavor with rosemary and coarse sea salt.

Makes 1 loaf

INGREDIENTS
3 cups unbleached all-purpose
    flour
½ tsp salt
2 tsp rapid-rise dried yeast
1 cup lukewarm water
3 tbsp olive oil
1 small red onion
leaves from 1 large rosemary sprig
1 tsp coarse sea salt

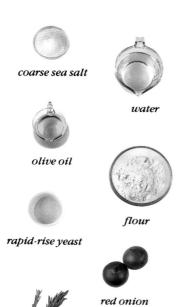

coarse sea salt

water

olive oil

flour

rapid-rise yeast

red onion

rosemary

1 Sift the flour and salt into a large mixing bowl. Stir in the yeast, then make a well in the center of the dry ingredients. Pour in the water and 2 tbsp of the oil. Mix well, adding a little more water if the mixture seems dry.

2 Turn the dough on to a lightly floured surface and knead for about 10 minutes until smooth and elastic.

3 Place the dough in a greased bowl, cover and let rise in a warm place for about 1 hour until doubled in size. Punch down and knead the dough for 2–3 minutes.

4 Meanwhile, preheat the oven to 425°F. Roll out the dough to a large circle, about ½ in thick, and transfer to a greased baking sheet. Brush with the remaining oil.

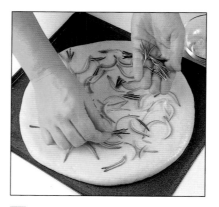

5 Halve the onion and slice into thin wedges. Sprinkle over the dough with the rosemary and sea salt, pressing in lightly.

6 Using a finger make deep indentations in the dough. Cover the surface with greased plastic wrap, then let rise in a warm place for 30 minutes. Remove the plastic wrap and bake for 25–30 minutes until golden. Serve warm.

Ham and Pineapple French Bread Pizza

French bread makes a great pizza base. For a really speedy recipe use ready-made pizza topping instead of the Tomato Sauce.

Serves 4

INGREDIENTS
2 small baguettes
1 quantity Tomato Sauce
3 oz sliced cooked ham
4 rings canned pineapple, drained
    well and chopped
½ small green bell pepper, seeded
    and cut into thin strips
3 oz sharp Cheddar
salt and black pepper

sharp Cheddar

green bell pepper

pineapple

cooked ham

baguette

Tomato Sauce

1 Preheat the oven to 400°F. Cut the baguettes in half lengthwise and toast the cut sides until crisp and golden.

2 Spread the Tomato Sauce over the toasted baguettes.

3 Cut the ham into strips and arrange on the baguettes with the pineapple and pepper. Season.

4 Grate the Cheddar and sprinkle on top. Bake or broil for 15–20 minutes until crisp and golden.

Prosciutto, Roasted Bell Peppers and Mozzarella Pizzas

Succulent roasted peppers, salty prosciutto and creamy mozzarella – the delicious flavors of these easy pizzas are hard to beat.

Serves 2

INGREDIENTS
½ loaf country bread
1 red bell pepper, roasted and peeled
1 yellow bell pepper, roasted and peeled
4 slices prosciutto, cut into thick strips
3 oz mozzarella
black pepper
tiny basil leaves, to garnish

country bread

basil

mozzarella

prosciutto

red and yellow bell peppers

1 Cut the bread into four thick slices and toast both sides until golden.

2 Cut the roasted peppers into thick strips and arrange on the toasted bread with the prosciutto.

3 Thinly slice the mozzarella and arrange on top. Grind plenty of black pepper over. Place under a hot broiler until the cheese is bubbling.

4 Arrange the basil leaves on top and serve immediately.

Spaghetti Olio e Aglio

This is a classic recipe from Rome. A quick and filling dish, originally the food of the poor involving nothing more than pasta, garlic and olive oil, but now fast becoming fashionable.

Serves 4

INGREDIENTS
2 garlic cloves
2 tbsp fresh parsley
½ cup olive oil
1 lb spaghetti
salt and pepper

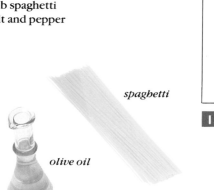

spaghetti

olive oil

parsley

garlic

1 Finely chop the garlic.

2 Chop the parsley roughly.

3 Heat the olive oil in a medium saucepan and add the garlic and a pinch of salt. Cook gently, stirring all the time, until golden. If the garlic becomes too brown, it will taste bitter.

4 Meanwhile cook the spaghetti in plenty of boiling salted water according to the manufacturer's instructions. Drain well.

5 Toss with the warm – not sizzling – garlic and oil and add plenty of black pepper and the parsley. Serve immediately.

Fiorentina Pizza

Spinach is the star ingredient of this pizza. A grating of nutmeg to heighten its flavor gives this pizza its unique character.

Serves 2–3

INGREDIENTS
6 oz fresh spinach
3 tbsp olive oil
1 small red onion, thinly sliced
1 pizza base, about 10–12 in
    diameter
1 quantity Tomato Sauce
freshly grated nutmeg
5 oz mozzarella
1 large egg
1 oz Gruyère, grated

mozzarella

Gruyère

Tomato Sauce

spinach

red onion

nutmeg

egg

1 Preheat the oven to 425°F. Remove the stems from the spinach and wash the leaves in plenty of cold water. Drain well and pat dry with paper towels.

2 Heat 1 tbsp of the oil and fry the onion until soft. Add the spinach and continue to fry until just wilted. Drain off any excess liquid.

3 Brush the pizza base with half the remaining oil. Spread over the Tomato Sauce, then top with the spinach mixture. Grate some nutmeg over.

4 Thinly slice the mozzarella and arrange over the spinach. Drizzle the remaining oil over. Bake for 10 minutes, then remove from the oven.

5 Make a small well in the center and drop the egg into the hole.

6 Sprinkle over the Gruyère and return to the oven for a further 5–10 minutes until crisp and golden. Serve immediately.

Mini Focaccia with Pine Nuts

Pine nuts add little bites of nutty texture to these mini focaccias.

Makes 4 mini loaves

INGREDIENTS
3 cups unbleached all-purpose
   flour
½ tsp salt
2 tsp rapid-rise dried yeast
1 cup lukewarm water
3 tbsp olive oil
3–4 tbsp pine nuts
2 tsp coarse sea salt

water

sea salt

olive oil

flour

rapid-rise yeast

pine nuts

1 Sift the flour and salt into a large mixing bowl. Stir in the yeast, then make a well in the center of the dry ingredients. Pour in the water and 2 tbsp of the oil. Mix well, adding more water if the mixture seems dry. Turn on to a lightly floured surface and knead for about 10 minutes until smooth and elastic. Place the dough in a greased bowl, cover and let rise in a warm place for about 1 hour until doubled in size. Punch down and knead the dough for 2–3 minutes.

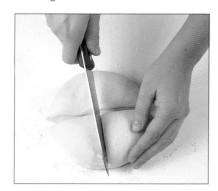

2 Divide the dough into four pieces.

3 Using your hands pat out each piece on greased baking sheets to a 4 × 3 in oblong, rounded at the ends.

4 Scatter the pine nuts over and gently press them into the surface. Sprinkle with salt and brush with the remaining oil. Cover with greased plastic wrap and let rise for about 30 minutes. Meanwhile, preheat the oven to 425°F. Remove the plastic wrap and bake the focaccias for 15–20 minutes until golden. Serve warm.

Walnut Bread

The nutty flavor of this wonderfully textured bread is excellent. Try it toasted and topped with melting goat cheese for a mouthwatering snack.

Makes 2 loaves

INGREDIENTS
4 cups bread flour
2 tsp salt
2 tsp rapid-rise dried yeast
1¼ cups chopped walnuts
4 tbsp chopped fresh parsley
1⅔ cups lukewarm water
4 tbsp olive oil

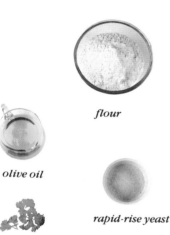

olive oil

flour

rapid-rise yeast

parsley

walnuts

salt

1 Sift the flour and salt into a large mixing bowl. Stir in the yeast, walnuts and parsley.

2 Make a well in the center of the dry ingredients. Pour in the water and oil and mix to a soft dough. Turn the dough on to a lightly floured surface and knead for about 10 minutes until smooth and elastic. Place in a greased bowl, cover and let rise in a warm place for about 1 hour until doubled in size.

3 Punch down and knead the dough for 2–3 minutes. Divide in half and shape each piece into a thick roll about 7–8 in long. Place on greased baking sheets, cover with plastic wrap and let rise for about 30 minutes.

4 Meanwhile, preheat the oven to 425°F. Remove the plastic wrap, then lightly slash the top of each loaf. Bake for 10 minutes, then reduce the oven temperature to 350°F. and bake for a further 25–30 minutes until the loaves sound hollow when tapped. Serve warm.

Quattro Stagioni Pizza

(Four Seasons)

This traditional pizza is divided into quarters, each with a different topping to depict the four seasons of the year.

Serves 2–4

INGREDIENTS

3 tbsp olive oil
2 oz mushrooms, sliced
1 pizza base, about 10–12 in
   diameter
1 quantity Tomato Sauce
2 oz prosciutto
6 pitted black olives, chopped
4 bottled artichoke hearts in oil,
   drained
3 canned anchovy fillets, drained
2 oz mozzarella, thinly sliced
8 fresh basil leaves, shredded
black pepper

artichoke hearts

mozzarella

olive oil

Tomato Sauce

prosciutto

basil

mushrooms

black olives

anchovy fillets

1 Preheat the oven to 425°F. Heat 1 tbsp of the oil in a frying pan and fry the mushrooms until all the juices have evaporated. Leave to cool.

2 Brush the pizza base with half the remaining oil. Spread over the Tomato Sauce and mark into four equal sections with a knife.

3 Arrange the mushrooms over one section of the pizza.

4 Cut the prosciutto into strips and arrange with the olives on another section.

5 Thinly slice the artichoke hearts and arrange over a third section. Halve the anchovies lengthwise and arrange with the mozzarella over the fourth section.

6 Sprinkle the basil over. Drizzle the remaining oil over and season with black pepper. Bake for 15–20 minutes until crisp and golden. Serve immediately.

Pasta with Roasted Bell Pepper and Tomato Sauce

Add other vegetables such as French beans or zucchini or even chick peas (garbanzos) to make this sauce more substantial.

Serves 4

INGREDIENTS
2 medium red bell peppers
2 medium yellow bell peppers
3 tbsp olive oil
1 medium onion, sliced
2 garlic cloves, crushed
½ tsp mild chili powder
14 oz canned chopped plum tomatoes
salt and pepper
4 cups dried pasta shells or spirals
freshly grated Parmesan cheese, to
    serve

bell peppers

pasta shells

onion

garlic

1 Preheat the oven to 400°F. Place the bell peppers on a baking sheet or in a roasting pan and bake for about 20 minutes or until beginning to char. Alternatively broil the peppers, turning frequently.

2 Rub the skins off the peppers under cold water. Halve, remove the seeds, and roughly chop the flesh.

3 Heat the oil in a medium saucepan and add the onion and garlic. Cook gently for 5 minutes until soft and golden.

4 Stir in the chili powder, cook for 2 minutes, then add the tomatoes and peppers. Bring to a boil and simmer for 10–15 minutes until slightly thickened and reduced. Season to taste.

5 Cook the pasta in plenty of boiling salted water according to the manufacturer's instructions. Drain well and toss with the sauce. Serve piping hot with lots of Parmesan cheese.

Leeks with Parsley, Egg, and Walnut Dressing

In French cooking, leeks are valued for their smooth texture as well as their flavor. They make a wonderful salad, which should be eaten slightly warm, so it is the ideal dish to serve with assorted pâtés and boiled new potatoes for a gourmet picnic feast.

Serves 4

INGREDIENTS
1½ lb young leeks
1 egg

DRESSING
1 oz fresh parsley
2 tbsp olive oil, preferably French
juice of ½ lemon
½ cup broken walnuts, toasted
1 tsp superfine sugar
salt and pepper

parsley

walnuts

leeks

egg

1 Bring a saucepan of salted water to a boil. Cut the leeks into 4 in lengths and rinse well to flush out any grit or soil. Cook the leeks for 8 minutes. Drain and part-cool under running water.

2 Lower the egg into boiling water and cook for 12 minutes. Cool under running water, shell, and set aside.

3 For the dressing, finely chop the parsley in a food processor.

4 Add the olive oil, lemon juice, and toasted walnuts. Blend for 1–2 minutes until smooth.

5 Adjust the consistency with about ⅓ cup water. Add the sugar and season to taste with salt and pepper.

6 Place the leeks on an attractive plate, then spoon on the sauce. Finely grate the hard-cooked egg and scatter over the sauce. Serve at room temperature.

Goat Cheese Salad with Buckwheat, Fresh Figs, and Walnuts

The robust flavors of goat cheese and buckwheat combine especially well with ripe figs and walnuts. The olive and nut oil dressing contains no vinegar and depends instead on the acidity of the cheese. Enjoy with a gutsy red wine from either the Rhône valley or South of France.

Serves 4

INGREDIENTS
¾ cup couscous
2 tbsp toasted buckwheat
1 egg, hard-cooked
2 tbsp chopped fresh parsley
4 tbsp olive oil, preferably Sicilian
3 tbsp walnut oil
4 oz arugula
½ frisée lettuce
about 1 cup crumbly white goat
    cheese
½ cup broken walnuts, toasted
4 ripe figs, trimmed and almost cut
    into four (leave the pieces joined at
    the base)

2 Shell the hard-cooked egg and pass it through a fine grater.

I Place the couscous and buckwheat in a bowl, cover with boiling water, and leave to soak for 15 minutes. Place in a strainer if necessary to drain off any remaining water, then spread out on a metal tray and allow to cool.

3 Toss the egg, parsley, and couscous in a bowl. Combine the two oils and use half to moisten the couscous mixture.

frisée lettuce

arugula

goat cheese

egg

figs

parsley

4 Wash and spin the salad leaves, dress with the remaining oil, and distribute between 4 large plates.

COOK'S TIP

Goat cheeses vary in strength from the youngest, which are soft and mild, to strongly flavored mature cheeses, that have a firm and crumbly texture. Crumbly cheeses are best for salads.

5 Pile the couscous in the center, crumble on the goat cheese, scatter with toasted walnuts, and add the figs.

Caesar Salad

There are many stories about the origin of Caesar Salad. The most likely is that it was invented by an Italian, Caesar Cardini, who owned a restaurant in Mexico in the 1920s. Simplicity is the key to its success.

Serves 4

INGREDIENTS
3 slices day-old bread, ½ in thick
4 tbsp garlic oil
salt and pepper
2 oz piece Parmesan cheese
1 romaine lettuce

DRESSING
2 egg yolks, as fresh as possible
1 oz canned anchovies, roughly
    chopped
½ tsp Dijon mustard
½ cup olive oil, preferably Italian
1 tbsp white-wine vinegar

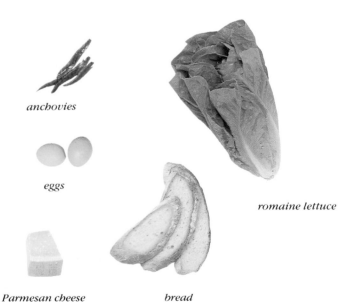

anchovies

eggs

romaine lettuce

Parmesan cheese   *bread*

COOK'S TIP

The classic dressing for Caesar Salad is made with raw egg yolks. Ensure you use only the freshest eggs, bought from a reputable dealer. Expectant mothers, young children and the elderly are not advised to eat raw egg yolks. You could omit them from the dressing and grate hard-cooked yolks on top of the salad instead.

1 To make the dressing, combine the egg yolks, anchovies, mustard, oil, and vinegar in a screw-top jar and shake well.

2 Remove the crusts from the bread with a serrated knife and cut into 1 in fingers.

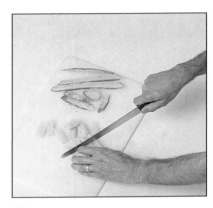

3 Heat the garlic oil in a large skillet, add the pieces of bread, and fry until golden. Sprinkle with salt and leave to drain on paper towels.

4 Cut thin shavings from the Parmesan cheese with a vegetable peeler.

5 Wash the salad leaves and spin dry. Smother with the dressing, and scatter with garlic croutons and Parmesan cheese. Season and serve.

Potato Salad with Egg and Lemon Dressing

Potato salads are a popular addition to any salad spread and are enjoyed with an assortment of cold meats and fish. This recipe draws on the contrasting flavors of egg and lemon. Chopped parsley provides a fresh finish.

Serves 4

INGREDIENTS
2 lb new potatoes, scrubbed or
    scraped
salt and pepper
1 medium onion, finely chopped
1 egg, hard-cooked
1¼ cups mayonnaise
1 clove garlic, crushed
finely grated zest and juice of 1 lemon
4 tbsp chopped fresh parsley

COOK'S TIP

At certain times of the year potatoes are inclined to fall apart when boiled. This usually coincides with the end of a particular season when potatoes become starchy. Early-season varieties are therefore best for making salads.

egg

garlic

onion

lemon

new potatoes

1 Bring the potatoes to a boil in a saucepan of salted water. Simmer for 20 minutes. Drain and allow to cool. Cut the potatoes into large dice, season well, and combine with the onion.

2 Shell the hard-cooked egg and grate into a mixing bowl, then add the mayonnaise. Combine the garlic and lemon zest and juice in a small bowl and stir into the mayonnaise.

3 Fold in the chopped parsley, mix thoroughly into the potatoes, and serve.

Tomato and Feta Cheese Salad

Sweet sun-ripened tomatoes are rarely more delicious than when served with feta cheese and olive oil. This salad, popular in Greece and Turkey, is enjoyed as a light meal with pieces of crispy bread.

Serves 4

INGREDIENTS
2 lb tomatoes
7 oz feta cheese
½ cup olive oil, preferably Greek
12 black olives
4 sprigs fresh basil
black pepper

COOK'S TIP

Feta cheese has a strong flavor and can be salty. The least salty variety is imported from Greece and Turkey, and is available from specialty or gourmet stores.

2 Slice the tomatoes thickly and arrange in a shallow dish.

3 Crumble the cheese over the tomatoes, sprinkle with olive oil, then sprinkle over the olives and fresh basil. Season with freshly ground black pepper and serve at room temperature.

1 Remove the tough cores from the tomatoes with a small knife.

tomatoes

basil

feta cheese

olives

Spicy Vegetable Fritters with Thai Salsa

The Thai salsa goes just as well with plain stir-fried salmon strips or stir-fried beef as it does with these zucchini fritters.

Serves 2–4 as a starter

INGREDIENTS
2 tsp cumin seeds
2 tsp coriander seeds
1 lb zucchini
1 cup chickpea (gram) flour
½ tsp baking soda
½ cup peanut oil
fresh mint sprigs, to garnish

FOR THE THAI SALSA
½ cucumber, diced
3 scallions, chopped
6 radishes, cubed
2 tbsp fresh mint, chopped
1 in piece ginger root, peeled and grated
3 tbsp lime juice
2 tbsp superfine sugar
3 cloves garlic, crushed

cucumber

mint ginger

radishes

zucchini

1 Heat the wok, then toast the cumin and coriander seeds. Cool them, then grind well, using a pestle and mortar.

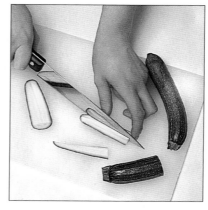

2 Cut the zucchini into 3 in sticks. Place in a bowl.

3 Blend the flour, baking soda, spices and salt and pepper in a food processor. Add ¼ cup warm water with 1 tbsp peanut oil, and blend again.

4 Coat the zucchini in the batter, then leave to stand for 10 minutes.

5 To make the Thai salsa, mix all the ingredients together in a bowl.

6 Heat the wok, then add the remaining oil. When the oil is hot, stir-fry the zucchini in batches. Drain well on paper towels, then serve hot with the salsa, garnished with fresh mint sprigs.

Tzatziki

Tzatziki is a Greek cucumber salad dressed with yogurt, mint, and garlic. It is typically served with grilled lamb and chicken, but is also good with salmon and trout.

Serves 4

INGREDIENTS
1 hothouse cucumber
1 tsp salt
3 tbsp finely chopped fresh mint, plus
  a few sprigs to garnish
1 clove garlic, crushed
1 tsp superfine sugar
scant 1 cup strained thick, Greek-style
  plain yogurt
paprika, to garnish (optional)

mint

cucumber

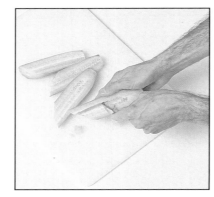

1 Peel the cucumber. Reserve a little to use as a garnish if you wish and cut the rest in half lengthwise. Remove the seeds with a teaspoon and discard. Slice the cucumber thinly and combine with salt. Leave for approximately 15–20 minutes. Salt will soften the cucumber and draw out any bitter juices.

2 Combine the mint, garlic, sugar, and yogurt in a bowl, reserving a few sprigs of mint as decoration.

3 Rinse the cucumber in a strainer under cold running water to remove the salt. Drain well and combine with the yogurt. Decorate with cucumber and mint. Serve cold. Tzatziki is traditionally garnished with paprika.

COOK'S TIP

If preparing Tzatziki in a hurry, leave out the method for salting cucumber at the end of step 1. The cucumber will have a more crunchy texture, and will be slightly less sweet.

Green Bean Salad with Egg Topping

When green beans are fresh and plentiful, serve them lightly cooked as a light entree topped with butter-fried bread crumbs, egg, and parsley.

Serves 4

INGREDIENTS

1½ lb green beans, trimmed and stringed
salt
2 tbsp garlic oil
1 oz butter
1 cup fresh white bread crumbs
4 tbsp chopped fresh parsley
1 egg, hard-cooked and shelled

parsley

egg

green beans

1 Bring a large saucepan of salted water to the boil. Add the beans and cook for 6 minutes. Drain well, toss in garlic oil, and allow to cool.

2 Heat the butter in a large skillet, add the bread crumbs, and fry until golden. Remove from the heat, add the parsley, then grate in the hard-cooked egg.

3 Place the beans in a shallow serving dish and spoon on the bread crumb topping. Serve at room temperature.

COOK'S TIP

Few cooks need reminding how to boil an egg, but many are faced with the problem of a dark ring around the yolk when cooked. This is caused by boiling for longer than the optimum period of 12 minutes. Allow boiled eggs to cool in water for easy peeling.

Fruit and Fiber Salad

Fresh, fast and filling, this salad makes a great starter, supper or snack.

Serves 4–6

INGREDIENTS
8 oz red or white cabbage or a
    mixture of both
3 medium carrots
1 pear
1 red-skinned apple
7 oz can lima beans,
    drained
¼ cup chopped dates

FOR THE DRESSING
½ tsp dry English mustard
2 tsp honey
2 tbsp orange juice
1 tsp white wine vinegar
½ tsp paprika
salt and freshly ground black pepper

carrot

dates

orange

lima
beans

cabbage

pear

apple

1 Shred the cabbage very finely, discarding any tough stalks.

2 Cut the carrots into very thin strips, about 2 in long.

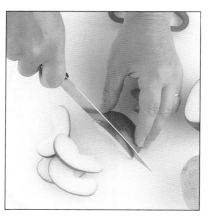

3 Quarter, core and slice the pear and apple, leaving the skin on.

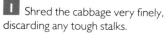

4 Put the fruit and vegetables in a bowl with the beans and dates. Mix well.

5 For the dressing, blend the mustard with the honey until smooth. Add the orange juice, vinegar, paprika and seasoning and mix well.

6 Pour the dressing over the salad and toss to coat. Chill in the refrigerator for 30 minutes before serving.

Mixed Roasted Vegetables

Frying Parmesan cheese in this unusual way gives a wonderful crusty coating to the vegetables and creates a truly Mediterranean flavor.

Serves 4 as an accompaniment

INGREDIENTS
1 large eggplant, about 8 oz
salt, for sprinkling
6 oz plum tomatoes
2 red peppers
1 yellow pepper
2 tbsp olive oil
1 oz Parmesan cheese
2 tbsp fresh parsley, chopped
freshly ground black pepper

peppers

plum tomatoes

eggplant

1 Cut the eggplant into segments lengthwise. Place in a colander and sprinkle with salt. Leave for 30 minutes, to allow the salt to draw out the bitter juices.

2 Rinse off the salt under cold water and pat dry on paper towels.

3 Cut the plum tomatoes into segments lengthwise.

4 Cut the red and yellow peppers into quarters lengthwise and deseed.

5 Heat the wok, then add 1 tsp of the olive oil. When the oil is hot, add the Parmesan and stir-fry until golden brown. Remove from the wok, allow to cool and chop into fine flakes.

6 Heat the wok, and then add the remaining oil. When the oil is hot stir-fry the eggplant and peppers for 4–5 minutes. Stir in the tomatoes and stir-fry for a further 1 minute. Toss the vegetables in the Parmesan, parsley and black pepper and serve.

Bulgur and Mint Salad with Fresh Vegetables

Also known as cracked wheat, burghul or pourgouri, the bulgur has been partially cooked, so it requires only a short soaking before serving.

Serves 4

INGREDIENTS
1⅔ cups bulgur
4 tomatoes
4 small zucchini, thinly sliced
   lengthwise
4 scallions, sliced on the diagonal
8 ready-to-eat dried apricots, chopped
¼ cup raisins
juice of 1 lemon
2 tbsp tomato juice
3 tbsp chopped fresh mint
1 garlic clove, crushed
salt and freshly ground black pepper
sprig of fresh mint, to garnish

zucchini

bulgur

tomatoes

lemon

scallions

1 Put the bulgur into a large bowl. Add enough cold water to come 1 in above the level of the wheat. Leave the bulgur to soak for 30 minutes, then drain well and squeeze out any excess water in a clean dish towel.

2 Meanwhile plunge the tomatoes into boiling water for 1 minute and then into cold water. Slip off the skins. Halve, remove the seeds and cores and roughly chop the flesh.

3 Stir the chopped tomatoes, sliced zucchini, scallions, apricots, and raisins into the bulgur.

4 Put the lemon and tomato juice, mint, garlic clove and seasoning into a small bowl and whisk together with a fork. Pour over the salad and mix well. Chill in the refrigerator for at least 1 hour. Serve garnished with a sprig of mint.

Cachumbar

Cachumbar is a salad relish most commonly served with Indian curries. There are many versions, although this one will leave your mouth feeling cool and refreshed after a spicy meal.

Serves 4

INGREDIENTS
3 ripe tomatoes
2 scallions, chopped
¼ tsp superfine sugar
salt
3 tbsp chopped fresh cilantro

tomatoes

cilantro

scallion

COOK'S TIP
Cachumbar also makes a fine accompaniment to fresh crab, lobster, and shellfish.

2 Halve the tomatoes, remove the seeds, and dice the flesh.

3 Combine the tomatoes with the scallions, sugar, salt, and chopped cilantro. Serve at room temperature.

1 Remove the tough cores from the tomatoes with a small knife.

Russian Salad

Russian salad became fashionable in the hotel dining rooms of Europe in the 1920s and 1930s. Originally it consisted of lightly cooked vegetables, eggs, shellfish, and mayonnaise. Today we find it diced in plastic tubs in supermarkets. This version recalls better days and plays on the theme of the Fabergé egg.

Serves 4

INGREDIENTS

¼ lb large button mushrooms
½ cup mayonnaise
1 tbsp lemon juice
12 oz cooked peeled shrimp
1 large dill pickle, chopped, or 2 tbsp capers
salt, pepper, and paprika
¼ lb fava beans
¼ lb small new potatoes, scrubbed or scraped
¼ lb young carrots, trimmed and peeled
¼ lb baby corn
¼ lb baby turnips, trimmed
1 tbsp olive oil, preferably French or Italian
4 eggs, hard-cooked and shelled
1 oz canned anchovies, cut into fine strips

1 Slice the mushrooms thinly, then cut into matchsticks. Combine the mayonnaise and lemon juice. Fold half of the mayonnaise into the mushrooms and shrimp, add the chopped dill pickle, then season to taste.

2 Bring a large saucepan of salted water to a boil, add the fava beans, and cook for 3 minutes. Drain and cool under running water, then pinch the beans between thumb and forefinger to release them from their tough skins. Boil the potatoes for 20 minutes and the remaining vegetables for 6 minutes. Drain and cool under running water.

3 Toss the vegetables with oil and divide between 4 shallow bowls. Spoon on the dressed shrimp and place a hard-cooked egg in the center. Decorate the egg with strips of anchovy and sprinkle with paprika.

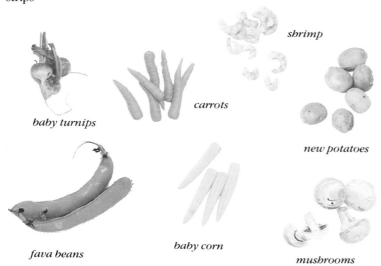

shrimp

carrots

baby turnips

new potatoes

fava beans

baby corn

mushrooms

Marinated Cucumber Salad

Sprinkling the cucumber with salt draws out some of the water and makes them crisper.

Serves 4–6

INGREDIENTS
2 medium cucumbers
1 tbsp salt
¼ cup sugar
¾ cup cider
1 tbsp cider vinegar
3 tbsp chopped fresh dill
pinch of pepper

cider

dill

sugar

vinegar

cucumber

1 Slice the cucumbers thinly and place them in a colander, sprinkling salt between each layer. Put the colander over a bowl and leave to drain for 1 hour.

2 Thoroughly rinse the cucumber under cold running water to remove excess salt, then pat dry on absorbent paper towels.

3 Gently heat the sugar, cider and vinegar in a saucepan, until the sugar has dissolved. Remove from the heat and leave to cool. Put the cucumber slices in a bowl, pour over the cider mixture and leave to marinate for 2 hours.

4 Drain the cucumber and sprinkle with the dill and pepper to taste. Mix well and transfer to a serving dish. Chill in the refrigerator until ready to serve.

Spinach and Potato Galette

Creamy layers of potato, spinach and herbs make a delicious supper dish.

Serves 6

INGREDIENTS
2 lb large potatoes
1 lb fresh spinach
2 eggs
14 oz (1¾ cups) low-fat cream
 cheese
1 tbsp grainy mustard
3 tbsp chopped fresh herbs (e.g.
 chives, parsley, chervil or sorrel)
salt and freshly ground black pepper

mustard
parsley
cream cheese
spinach
egg
potatoes
chives
cherry tomatoes
chervil
sorrel

COOK'S TIP

Choose firm white or red skinned
boiling potatoes for this dish.

1 Preheat the oven to 350°F. Line a deep 9 in cake pan with parchment paper. Place the potatoes in a large pot and cover with cold water. Bring to a boil and cook for 10 minutes. Drain well and allow to cool slightly before peeling and slicing thinly.

2 Wash the spinach well and place in a large pot with only the water that is clinging to the leaves. Cover and cook, stirring once, until the spinach has just wilted. Drain well in a sieve and squeeze out the excess moisture Chop finely.

3 Beat the eggs with the cream cheese and mustard then stir in the chopped spinach and fresh herbs.

4 Place a layer of the sliced potatoes in the lined pan, arranging them in concentric circles. Top with a spoonful of the cream cheese mixture and spread out. Continue layering, seasoning with salt and pepper as you go, until all the potatoes and the cream cheese mixture are used up.

5 Cover the pan with a piece of foil and place in a roasting pan.

6 Fill the roasting pan with enough boiling water to come halfway up the sides, and cook in the oven for 45–50 minutes. Turn out onto a plate and serve hot or cold.

Eggplant, Roast Garlic and Red Pepper Pâté

This is a simple pâté of smoky baked eggplant, sweet pink peppercorns and red peppers, with more than a hint of garlic!

Serves 4

INGREDIENTS
3 medium eggplants
2 red peppers
5 whole garlic cloves
1½ tsp pink peppercorns in brine, drained and crushed
2 tbsp chopped fresh coriander

eggplant

garlic

coriander

pink peppercorns

red pepper

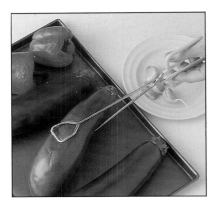

1 Preheat the oven to 400°F. Arrange the whole eggplants, peppers and garlic cloves on a cookie sheet and place in the oven. After 10 minutes remove the garlic cloves and turn over the eggplants and peppers.

2 Peel the garlic cloves and place in the bowl of a blender.

3 After a further 20 minutes remove the blistered and charred peppers from the oven and place in a paper bag. Leave to cool.

4 After a further 10 minutes remove the eggplants from the oven. Split in half and scoop the flesh into a sieve placed over a bowl. Press the flesh with a spoon to remove the bitter juices.

5 Add the mixture to the garlic in the blender and blend until smooth. Place in a large mixing bowl.

6 Peel and chop the red peppers and stir into the eggplant mixture. Mix in the peppercorns and fresh coriander and serve at once.

Raspberry and Passionfruit Puffs

Few desserts are so strikingly easy to make as this one: beaten egg whites and sugar baked in a dish, turned out and served with a handful of soft fruit.

VARIATION
If raspberries are out of season, use either fresh, bottled or canned soft berry fruit such as strawberries, blueberries or red currants.

Serves 4

INGREDIENTS
2 tbsp butter, softened
5 egg whites
⅔ cup superfine sugar
2 passionfruit
1 cup ready-made custard from a
   carton or can
milk, as required
6 cups fresh raspberries
confectioners' sugar, for dusting

raspberries

egg whites

passionfruit

confectioners' sugar

1 Preheat the oven to 350°F. Brush four ½ pint soufflé dishes with a visible layer of soft butter.

2 Whisk the egg whites in a mixing bowl until firm. (You can use an electric mixer.) Add the sugar a little at a time and whisk into a firm meringue.

3 Halve the passionfruit, take out the seeds with a spoon and fold them into the meringue.

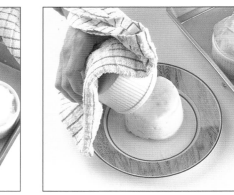

4 Turn the meringue out into the prepared dishes, stand in a deep roasting pan which has been half-filled with boiling water and bake for 10 minutes. The meringue will rise above the tops of the soufflé dishes.

5 Turn the puffs out upside-down onto a serving plate.

6 Top with raspberries. Thin the custard with a little milk and pour around the edge. Dredge with confectioners' sugar and serve warm or cold.

Red Fruit Fool

This delicious fruity dessert would be ideal for a summer lunch.

Serves 4

INGREDIENTS
1 lb mixed red fruit, such as
  raspberries, red currants and
  strawberries
2 tsp fructose
½ tsp arrowroot
⅔ cup low fat whipping
  cream
1 tsp vanilla extract
fresh fruit, to decorate

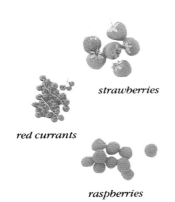

strawberries

red currants

raspberries

1 Put the fruit and fructose into a large heavy-based saucepan and simmer over a low heat for 2 minutes, or until just soft.

2 Blend the arrowroot with 2 tsp cold water. Add to the fruit and simmer for a further minute, or until thickened. Cool and chill in the refrigerator for I hour.

3 Divide two-thirds of the fruit mixture between four individual glasses.

4 Purée the rest of the fruit and strain through a fine sieve to remove the seeds.

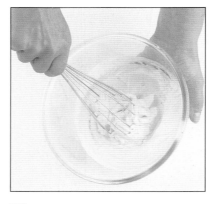

5 Lightly whip the cream and vanilla extract together until soft peaks form. Fold in the remaining fruit purée.

6 Spoon the fruit cream mixture between the glasses and chill for 30 minutes. Serve decorated with fresh fruit.

COOK'S TIP

Fructose is a natural fruit sugar. It is slightly sweeter than granulated sugar (sucrose) so less is needed. If you use granulated sugar instead, use 1 tbsp for this recipe.

Mandarins in Orange-flower Syrup

Mandarins, tangerines, clementines, mineolas: any of these lovely citrus fruits are suitable for this recipe.

Serves 4

INGREDIENTS
10 mandarins
1 tbsp confectioner's sugar
2 tsp orange-flower water
1 tbsp chopped pistachio nuts

orange-flower water

pistachio nuts

mandarines

confectioner's sugar

COOK'S TIP
The mandarins look very attractive if you leave them whole, especially if there is a large quantity for a special occasion, but you may prefer to separate the segments.

1 Thinly pare a little of the colored rind from one mandarin and cut it into fine shreds for decoration. Squeeze the juice from two mandarins and reserve it.

2 Peel the remaining fruit, removing as much of the white pith as possible. Arrange the whole fruit in a wide dish.

3 Mix the reserved juice, sugar and orange-flower water and pour it over the fruit. Cover the dish and chill for at least an hour.

4 Blanch the shreds of rind in boiling water for 30 seconds. Drain, leave to cool and sprinkle them over the mandarins, with the pistachio nuts, to serve.

Red Currant Filo Baskets

Filo pastry is light as air and makes a very elegant dessert. It's also low in fat and it needs only a fine brushing of oil before use: a light oil such as sunflower is the best choice for this recipe.

Serves 6

INGREDIENTS
3 sheets filo pastry (about
    3½ oz)
1 tbsp sunflower oil
1½ cups red currants
1 cup strained plain yogurt
1 tsp confectioner's sugar

filo pastry

yogurt

red currants

sunflower oil

confectioner's sugar

I Preheat the oven to 400°F. Cut the sheets of filo pastry into 18 squares with sides about 4 in long.

2 Brush each filo square very thinly with oil, and then arrange the squares overlapping in six small tartlette pans, layering them in threes. Bake for 6–8 minutes, until crisp and golden. Lift the baskets out carefully and let them cool on a wire rack.

VARIATION

Strawberries or raspberries can be substituted for red currants, if they are not available.

3 Reserve a few sprigs of red currants on their stems for decoration and string the rest. Stir the currants into the yogurt.

4 Spoon the yogurt into the filo baskets. Decorate them with the reserved sprigs of red currants and sprinkle them with confectioner's sugar.

Tofu Berry 'Cheesecake'

This summery 'cheesecake' is a very light and refreshing finish to any meal. Strictly speaking, it's not a cheesecake at all, as it's based on tofu – but who would guess?

Serves 6

INGREDIENTS
FOR THE BASE
4 tbsp low-fat spread
2 tbsp apple juice
2½ cups bran flakes or other high-fiber cereal

FOR THE FILLING
1½ cups tofu or skim-milk soft cheese
⅞ cup low-fat plain yogurt
1 tbsp/1 packet powdered gelatin
4 tbsp apple juice

FOR THE TOPPING
1¾ cups fresh mixed summer soft fruit, e.g. strawberries, raspberries, red currants, blackberries, etc (or a mix of any of these frozen)
2 tbsp red currant jelly
2 tbsp hot water

apple juice

bran flakes

summer fruit

tofu

1 For the base, place the low-fat spread and apple juice in a pan and heat them gently until the spread has melted. Crush the cereal and stir it into the pan.

2 Tip into a 9 in round quiche pan and press down firmly. Leave to set.

3 For the filling, place the tofu or cheese and yogurt in a food processor and process them until smooth. Dissolve the gelatin in the apple juice and stir the juice quickly into the tofu mixture.

4 Spread the tofu mixture over the chilled base, smoothing it evenly. Chill until the filling has set.

5 Remove the quiche pan and place the 'cheesecake' on a serving plate.

6 Arrange the red fruits over the top. Melt the red currant jelly with the hot water. Let it cool, and then spoon over the fruit to serve.

Mango and Lime Sorbet in Lime Shells

This tartly flavored sorbet looks pretty served in the lime shells, but is also good served in scoops for a more traditional presentation.

Serves 4

INGREDIENTS
4 large limes
1 medium-size ripe mango
½ tbsp powdered gelatin
2 egg whites
1 tbsp granulated artificial sweetener
lime rind strips, to decorate

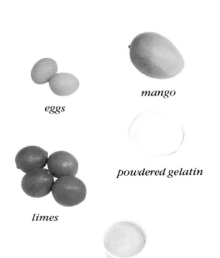

eggs

mango

powdered gelatin

limes

granulated artificial sweetener

COOK'S TIP

If you have lime juice left over from this recipe, it will freeze well for future use. Pour it into a small freezer container, seal it and freeze for up to six months. Or freeze it in useful measured amounts; pour 1 tbsp into each compartment of an ice-cube tray and freeze the tray.

1 Cut a thick slice from the top of each of the limes, and then cut a thin slice from the bottom end so that the limes will stand upright. Squeeze out the juice from the limes. Use a small knife to remove all the membrane from the center.

2 Halve, pit, peel and chop the mango and purée the flesh in a food processor with 2 tbsp of the lime juice. Dissolve the gelatine in 3 tbsp of lime juice and stir it into the mango mixture.

3 Whisk the egg whites until they hold soft peaks. Whisk in the sweetener. Fold the egg white mixture quickly into the mango mixture. Spoon the sorbet into the lime shells. Any leftover sorbet that will not fit into the lime shells can be frozen in small ramekins.

4 Place the filled shells in the freezer until the sorbet is firm. Cover the shells with plastic wrap. Before serving, allow the shells to stand at room temperature for about 10 minutes; decorate them with strips of lime rind.

Rhubarb and Orange Granita

Pretty pink rhubarb, with sweet oranges and honey – the perfect sweet ice.

Serves 4

INGREDIENTS
12 oz pink rhubarb
1 medium-size orange
1 tbsp honey
1 tsp powdered gelatin
orange slices, to decorate

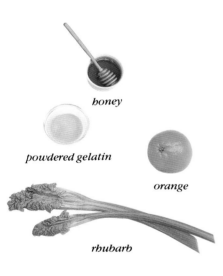

honey

powdered gelatin

orange

rhubarb

1 Trim the rhubarb and slice into 1 in lengths. Place the rhubarb in a pan.

2 Finely grate the rind from the orange and squeeze out the juice. Add about half the orange juice and the grated rind to the rhubarb in the pan and allow to simmer until the rhubarb is just tender. Stir in the honey.

3 Heat the remaining orange juice and stir in the gelatin to dissolve. Stir it into the rhubarb. Pour the whole mixture into a rigid freezer container and freeze it until it's slushy, about 2 hours.

4 Remove the mixture from the freezer and beat it well to break up the ice crystals. Return the granita to the freezer and freeze it again until firm. Allow the granita to soften slightly at room temperature before serving.

COOK'S TIP

Most pink, forced rhubarb is naturally quite sweet, but if yours is not, you can add a little more honey, sugar or artificial sweetener to taste.

Summer Fruit Salad Ice Cream

What could be more cooling on a hot summer day than fresh summer fruits, lightly frozen in this irresistible ice?

Serves 6

INGREDIENTS
2 lb/4½ cups mixed soft summer
  fruit, such as raspberries,
  strawberries, black currants, red
  currants, etc
2 eggs
1 cup plain strained yogurt
¾ cup red grape juice
1 tbsp/1 packet powdered gelatin

red grape juice

powdered gelatin

plain yogurt

eggs

summer fruits

COOK'S TIP
Red grape juice has a good flavor and improves the color of the ice, but if it is not available, use cranberry, apple or orange juice instead.

1 Reserve half the fruit and purée the rest in a food processor, or rub it through a sieve to make a smooth purée.

2 Separate the eggs and whisk the yolks and the yogurt into the fruit purée.

3 Heat the grape juice until it's almost boiling, and then remove it from the heat. Sprinkle the gelatin over the grape juice and stir to dissolve the gelatin completely.

4 Whisk the dissolved gelatin mixture into the fruit purée and then pour the mixture into a freezer container. Freeze until half-frozen and slushy in consistency.

5 Whisk the egg whites until they are stiff. Quickly fold them into the half-frozen mixture.

6 Return to the freezer and freeze until almost firm. Scoop into individual dishes or glasses and add the reserved soft fruits.

Watermelon, Ginger and Grapefruit Salad

This pretty, pink combination is very light and refreshing for any summer meal.

Serves 4

INGREDIENTS
1 lb/2 cups diced watermelon flesh
2 ruby or pink grapefruit
2 pieces preserved ginger in syrup
2 tbsp preserved ginger syrup

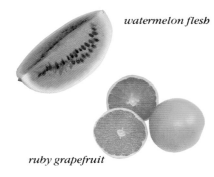

watermelon flesh

ruby grapefruit

preserved ginger in syrup

COOK'S TIP

Toss the fruits gently – grapefruit segments will break up easily and the appearance of the dish will be spoiled.

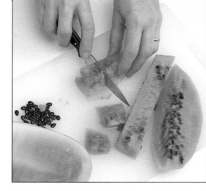

1 Remove any seeds from the watermelon and cut into bite-sized chunks.

2 Using a small sharp knife, cut away all the peel and white pith from the grapefruits and carefully lift out the segments, catching any juice in a bowl.

3 Finely chop the ginger and place in a serving bowl with the melon cubes and grapefruit segments, adding the reserved juice.

4 Spoon over the ginger syrup and toss the fruits lightly to mix evenly. Chill before serving.

Broiled Nectarines with Spiced Ricotta

This easy dessert makes a perfect end to a summer meal. Canned peach halves can also be used.

Serves 4

INGREDIENTS
4 ripe nectarines or peaches
1 tbsp light brown sugar
½ cup ricotta cheese or fromage frais
½ tsp ground star anise

nectarines

light brown sugar

ricotta cheese

ground star anise

1 Cut the nectarines in half and remove the pits.

2 Arrange the nectarines, cut-side upwards, in a wide flameproof dish or on a baking sheet.

COOK'S TIP
Star anise has a warm, rich flavor – if you can't get it, try ground cloves or ground allspice instead.

3 Stir the sugar into the ricotta or fromage frais. Using a teaspoon, spoon the mixture into the hollow of each nectarine half.

4 Sprinkle with the star anise. Place under a moderately hot broiler for 6–8 minutes, or until the nectarines are hot and bubbling. Serve warm.

Lemon Hearts with Strawberry Sauce

These elegant little hearts are light as air, and they are best made the day before your dinner party – which saves on last-minute panics as well!

Serves 6

INGREDIENTS
FOR THE HEARTS
¾ cup ricotta cheese
⅔ cup crème fraîche or sour cream
1 tbsp granulated artificial sweetener
finely grated rind of ½ lemon
2 tbsp lemon juice
2 tsp powdered gelatin
2 egg whites

FOR THE SAUCE
2 cups fresh or frozen and thawed
    strawberries
1 tbsp lemon juice

ricotta cheese

crème fraîche

powdered gelatin

lemon

strawberries

eggs

granulated artificial sweetener

1 Beat the ricotta cheese until smooth. Stir in the crème fraîche, sweetener and lemon rind.

2 Place the lemon juice in a small bowl and sprinkle the gelatin over it. Place the bowl over a pan of hot water and stir to dissolve the gelatin completely.

3 Quickly stir the gelatin into the cheese mixture, mixing it in evenly.

4 Beat the egg whites until they form soft peaks. Quickly fold them into the cheese mixture.

5 Spoon the mixture into six lightly oiled, individual heart-shaped molds and chill the moulds until set.

VARIATION

These little heart-shaped desserts are the perfect choice for a romantic dinner, but they don't have to be heart-shaped – try setting the mixture in individual fluted molds, or even in ordinary teacups.

6 Place the strawberries and lemon juice in a blender and process until smooth. Pour the sauce on to serving plates and place the turned-out hearts on top. Decorate with slices of strawberry.

Minted Raspberry Bavarois

A sophisticated dessert that can be made a day in advance for a special dinner party.

Serves 6

INGREDIENTS
5½ cups fresh or frozen and thawed
  raspberries
2 tbsp confectioner's sugar
2 tbsp lemon juice
1 tbsp finely chopped fresh mint
2 tbsp/2 packets powdered
  gelatin
5 tbsp boiling water
1¼ cups custard, made with
  skim milk
1⅛ cups strained plain yogurt
fresh mint sprigs, to decorate

skim-milk custard

confectioner's sugar

yogurt

powdered gelatin

lemon

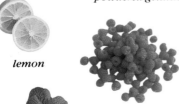
mint   *raspberries*

COOK'S TIP
You can make this dessert using frozen raspberries, which have a good color and flavor. Allow them to thaw at room temperature, and use any juice in the gelatin.

1 Reserve a few raspberries for decoration. Place the raspberries, icing sugar and lemon juice in a food processor and process them until smooth.

2 Press the purée through a sieve to remove the raspberry seeds. Add the mint. You should have about 2½ cups of purée.

3 Sprinkle 1 tsp of the gelatin over 2 tbsp of the boiling water and stir until the gelatin has dissolved. Stir into ⅔ cup of the fruit purée.

4 Pour this gelatin into a 4-cup mold, and leave the mold to chill in the refrigerator until it is just on the point of setting. Tip the mold to swirl the setting gelatin around the sides, and then leave to chill until the gelatin has set completely.

5 Stir the remaining fruit purée into the custard and yogurt. Dissolve the rest of the gelatin in the remaining water and stir it in quickly.

6 Pour the raspberry custard into the mold and let it chill until it has set completely. To serve, dip the mold quickly into hot water and then turn it out and decorate it with the reserved raspberries and the mint sprigs.

Cool Green Fruit Salad

A sophisticated, simple fruit salad for the summer.

Serves 6

INGREDIENTS
3 Honeydew melons
4 oz green seedless grapes
2 kiwi fruit
1 starfruit
1 green-skinned apple
1 lime
¾ cup sparkling white grape juice

grape juice

melons

seedless grapes

kiwi fruit

starfruit

lime

green-skinned apple

1 Cut the melons in half and scoop out the seeds. Keeping the shells intact, scoop out the flesh with a melon baller, or scoop it out with a spoon and cut into bite-size cubes. Reserve the melon shells.

2 Remove any stems from the grapes, and, if they are large, cut them in half. Peel and chop the kiwi fruit. Thinly slice the starfruit. Core and thinly slice the apple and place the slices in a bowl, with the melon, grapes, kiwi fruit and starfruit.

3 Thinly pare the rind from the lime and cut it in fine strips. Blanch the strips in boiling water for 30 seconds, and then drain them and rinse them in cold water. Squeeze the juice from the lime and toss it into the fruit.

4 Spoon the prepared fruit into the reserved melon shells and chill the shells in the refrigerator until required. Just before serving, spoon the sparkling grape juice over the fruit and sprinkle it with the lime rind.

COOK'S TIP

If you're serving this dessert on a hot summer day, serve the filled melon shells nestling on a platter of crushed ice to keep them beautifully cool.

Red Berry Sponge Tart

When soft berry fruits are in season, try making this delicious sponge tart. Serve warm from the oven with scoops of vanilla ice cream.

Serves 4

INGREDIENTS
softened butter, for greasing
4 cups soft berry fruits such as raspberries, blackberries, black currants, red currants, strawberries or blueberries
2 eggs, at room temperature
¼ cup superfine sugar, plus extra to taste (optional)
1 tbsp flour
¾ cup ground almonds
vanilla ice cream, to serve

eggs

ground almonds

flour

superfine sugar

red currants

black currants

raspberries   *strawberries*

1 Preheat the oven to 375°F. Brush a 9 in pic pan with softened butter and line the bottom with a circle of non-stick baking paper. Scatter the fruit in the bottom of the pan with a little sugar if the fruits are tart.

2 Whisk the eggs and sugar together for about 3–4 minutes or until they leave a thick trail across the surface. Combine the flour and almonds, then fold into the egg mixture with a spatula – retaining as much air as possible.

3 Spread the mixture on top of the fruit base and bake in the preheated oven for 15 minutes. Turn out onto a serving plate and serve with vanilla ice cream.

VARIATION

When berry fruits are out of season, use bottled fruits, but ensure that they are well drained before use.

Strawberry Rose Petal Pashka

This lighter version of a traditional Russian dessert is ideal for dinner parties – make it a day or two in advance for best results.

Serves 4

INGREDIENTS
1½ cups cottage cheese
¾ cup low-fat plain yogurt
2 tbsp honey
½ tsp rosewater
2½ cups strawberries
handful of scented pink rose petals, to decorate

honey

cottage cheese

rosewater

strawberries

yogurt

COOK'S TIP

The flowerpot shape is traditional for pashka, but you could make it in any shape – the small porcelain heart-shaped molds with draining holes usually used for *coeurs à la crème* make a pretty alternative.

1 Drain any liquid from the cottage cheese and pour the cheese into a sieve. Use a wooden spoon to rub it through the sieve into a bowl.

2 Stir the yogurt, honey and rose-water into the cheese.

3 Coarsely chop about half the strawberries and stir them into the cheese mixture.

4 Line a new, clean flowerpot or a sieve with fine cheesecloth and tip the cheese mixture in. Leave it to drain over a bowl for several hours, or overnight.

5 Invert the flowerpot or sieve on to a serving plate, turn out the pashka and remove the cheesecloth.

6 Decorate with the reserved strawberries and rose petals. Serve chilled.

Papaya Skewers with Passionfruit Sauce

Tropical fruits, full of natural sweetness, make a simple, exotic dessert.

Serves 6

INGREDIENTS
3 ripe papayas
10 passionfruit or kiwi fruit
2 tbsp lime juice
2 tbsp confectioner's sugar
2 tbsp white rum
toasted coconut, to garnish (optional)

confectioner's sugar

papayas

passionfruit

lime

COOK'S TIP

If you are short of time, the passion-fruit flesh can be used as it is, without puréeing or sieving. Simply scoop the flesh from the skins and mix it with the lime, sugar and rum. Kiwi fruit will still need to be puréed, however.

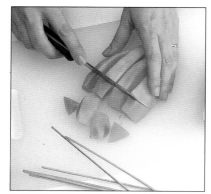

1 Cut the papayas in half and scoop out the seeds. Peel them and cut the flesh into even-size chunks. Thread the chunks on to six bamboo skewers.

2 Halve eight of the passionfruit or kiwi fruit and scoop out the flesh. Purée the flesh for a few seconds in a blender or food processor.

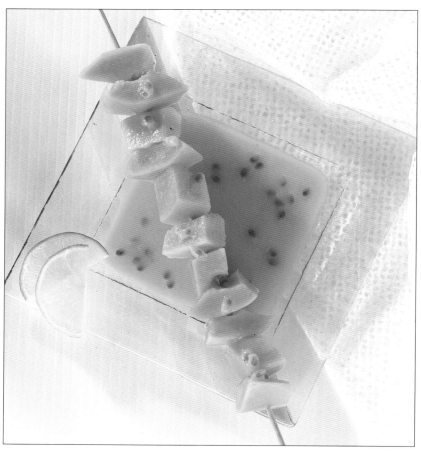

3 Press the pulp through a sieve and discard the seeds. Add the lime juice, sugar and rum, and then stir well until the sugar has dissolved.

4 Spoon a little sauce on to six serving plates. Place the skewers on top. Scoop the flesh from the remaining passion-fruit or kiwi fruit and spoon it over. Sprinkle with a little toasted coconut, if you like, and serve.

Figs with Ricotta Cream

Fresh, ripe figs are full of natural sweetness, and need little adornment. This simple recipe makes the most of their beautiful, intense flavor.

Serves 4

INGREDIENTS
4 ripe, fresh figs
½ cup ricotta or cottage cheese
3 tbsp crème fraîche
1 tbsp honey
½ tsp vanilla extract
freshly grated nutmeg, to decorate

vanilla extract

honey

crème fraîche

ricotta cheese

figs

nutmeg

COOK'S TIP
If you prefer, the honey can be omitted and replaced with a little artificial sweetener.

1 Trim the stalks from the figs. Make four cuts through each fig from the stalk-end, cutting them almost through but leaving them joined at the base.

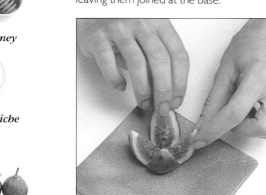

2 Place the figs on serving plates and open them out.

3 Mix together the ricotta or cottage cheese, crème fraîche, honey and vanilla.

4 Spoon a little ricotta cream on to each plate and sprinkle with grated nutmeg to serve.

Fresh Citrus Gelatin Mold

Fresh fruit gelatin molds really are worth the effort – they're packed with fresh flavor, natural color and vitamins – and they make a stunning fat-free dessert.

Serves 4

INGREDIENTS
3 medium-size oranges
1 lemon
1 lime
1¼ cups water
⅓ cup raw sugar
1 tbsp/1 packet powdered gelatin
extra slices of fruit, to decorate

powdered gelatin

raw sugar

lime

oranges

lemon

1 With a sharp knife, cut all the peel and white pith from one orange and carefully remove the segments. Arrange the segments in the base of a 3¾-cup mold or dish.

2 Remove some shreds of citrus rind with a zester and reserve them for decoration. Grate the remaining rind from the lemon and lime and one orange. Place all the grated rind in a pan, with the water and sugar.

3 Heat gently until the sugar has dissolved, without boiling. Remove from the heat. Squeeze the juice from all the rest of the fruit and stir it into the pan.

4 Strain the liquid into a measuring cup to remove the rind (you should have about 2½ cups: if necessary, make up the amount with water). Sprinkle the gelatin over the liquid and stir until it has completely dissolved.

5 Pour a little of the gelatin liquid over the orange segments and chill until set. Let the remaining liquid cool at room temperature, but do not allow it to set.

COOK'S TIP

To speed up the setting of the fruit segments in liquid, stand the dish in a bowl of ice. Or, if you're in a hurry, simply stir the segments into the liquid gelatin, pour into a serving dish and set it all together.

6 Pour the remaining cooled liquid into the dish and chill until set. To serve, turn out the mold and decorate it with the reserved citrus rind shreds and slices of citrus fruit.

INDEX